The

Maverick

Spirit

GEORGIA-PACIFIC AT 75

The

Maverick

Spirit

GEORGIA-PACIFIC AT 75

Doug Monroe

GREENWICH PUBLISHING GROUP, INC.
LYME, CONNECTICUT

Georgia-Pacific

Printed and bound in the United States of America. No part of this publication may be reproduced or transmitted in any form or by any means, electronic or mechanical, including photocopying, recording or any information storage and retrieval system now known or to be invented, without permission in writing from Georgia-Pacific Corp., Corporate Marketing, 133 Peachtree Street NE, Atlanta, GA 30303, except by a reviewer who wishes to quote brief passages in connection with a review written for inclusion in a magazine, newspaper or broadcast.

Produced and published by Greenwich Publishing Group, Inc. Lyme, Connecticut

Design by Clare Cunningham Graphic Design

Library of Congress Control Number: 2001096864

ISBN: 0-944641-51-2

First Printing: October 2001

The following are trademarks or registered trademarks of Georgia-Pacific Corporation and its subsidiaries: Quilted Northern, Angel Soft, MD, Brawny, Sparkle, Mardi Gras, Dixie, So-Dri, Soft 'n Gentle, Vanity Fair, Health Smart, Unisource and design, Nice 'n Soft, Spectrum, Green Forest, ToughRock, Dens-Glass Gold, and "We make the things that make you feel at home." Coronet is a former registered trademark of the company. Other marks are the property of their respective owners.

Photography Credits:

All images and artifacts appear courtesy of Georgia-Pacific Corporation except the following: p. 30 appears courtesy of C. Kinsey; p. 83 (lower right) reprinted from The Wall Street Journal, © 2001 Dow Jones & Company, Inc. All rights reserved.; p. 96 appears courtesy of The News Observer; p. 129 appears courtesy of Terrell Marett; and p. 155 appears courtesy of Harald Sund.

The oil landscape on page 15 is by Jim Palmer. The oil portraits on pages 33, 85, 121 and 145 are by Everett Raymond Kinstler.

Contents

CHAPTER ONE

The Courage to Change

Whenever he needed to think about the future, Alston D. "Pete" Correll Jr. took long walks on the beach at his vacation home on Sea Island, a barrier island off the southeast coast of Georgia. The empty stretch of windswept dunes lined with sea oats was his personal think tank, the perfect refuge from his office on the 51st floor of the Georgia-Pacific Corporation headquarters over-looking downtown Atlanta or the din in one of the company's gigantic paper mills.

An oil landscape in the Atlanta office of Georgia-Pacific Corporation Chairman and CEO Alston D. "Pete" Correll captures the view from his Sea Island retreat of the famed Marshes of Glynn County, immortalized by the Georgia poet Sidney Lanier. The marshes connect to a series of tidal rivers separating Sea Island from the blue-collar town of Brunswick, Georgia, where Correll grew up. It was at Sea Island that Correll decided to return Georgia-Pacific to its legendary roots as a maverick in the forest products industry.

On the beach, there were no jangling phones, no meetings, no roaring paper machines the size of football fields. It was just Correll and his four decades of experience in the forest products industry — and a stick to sketch his thoughts in the sand.

On a muggy summer day in 1997, Correll was driven to the beach out of sheer frustration. He was trying to figure out a way to reinvent Georgia-Pacific, to shake it loose from Wall Street perceptions that did not credit the company with its efficiencies and improvements and to break away from the swift-moving cycles that seemed to rush dark clouds over every step forward. He was looking for something far deeper than a minor shift in business practices. He was trying to foment a full-scale revolution in a rock-solid,

conservative organization. Most of all, Correll wanted to jumpstart the company out of the doldrums of conformity and return to the heady days when Georgia-Pacific was known by a single word — "maverick."

The significance of the beach where he brainstormed about the future of G-P was not lost on him. Sea Island, once home to playwright Eugene O'Neill, is one of America's most exclusive resorts. Yet Correll's island retreat was only a 15-minute drive from where he grew up, dirt poor, in the working-class coastal town of Brunswick, Georgia. The blue-collar town is separated from the white-tie resort by a small tidal river, the Mackay.

"My mother used to say, 'Honey, that's the widest river in the world,'" Correll recalls. "The trip from Brunswick to Sea Island is a much farther distance than any other I've traveled," he says.

Correll was 12 when his father died, leaving the boy and his mother to run Correll's Men Store in Brunswick and scrape out a modest living. Alston D. Correll Sr. had been nicknamed Pete as well but never explained the origin of the nickname to "Little Pete."

Correll and his mother kept the store running, with the hardworking young man learning to sew hems when they could not afford a seamstress. Correll keeps $1.50 neckties from the store framed in his office to remind him of his origins.

"My mother proved that if you work long enough and hard enough, you'll be all right," Correll says. "I learned very early in life that I can accomplish more in twelve hours than most people can in eight."

Correll's mother wanted the boy to have the presence of men in his life. She enrolled him in golf lessons at the Brunswick Country Club, on the working-class side of the river. Playing in the early mornings with the caddies, he became good enough to win a golf scholarship to Georgia Tech, but he was unhappy at the engineering school, with its mandatory slide rules and serious lack of women students.

After a stint as a runner for Merrill Lynch on the floor of the New York Stock Exchange, Correll decided to attend Tech's rival school, the University of Georgia, where he earned a business degree. He worked for J.C. Penney in Brunswick and stayed there until one night he found himself waiting on a customer who stayed a half-hour after the store's normal closing hours trying to make up his mind between two $2.98 shirts.

"My wife, Ada Lee, was sitting in the car, waiting for me, and I said, 'Honey, there has to be an easier way to make a living than this,'" Correll says. His mother suggested they move to her hometown of Covington, Virginia.

"I said, 'There's nothing to do in Covington but work for Westvaco.'" Suddenly, it seemed like a good idea. He called the company, and they hired him. Pete Correll was now in the paper industry, and he immediately took to the business, which drew from his practical retail experience and his innate gift for engineering.

After less than a year at Westvaco, he decided to go to graduate school, choosing the University of Maine over Harvard Business School. Despite the cachet of a Harvard M.B.A., Correll took the road less traveled

"My mother proved that if you work long enough and hard enough, you'll be all right," Correll says. "I learned very early in life that I can accomplish more in twelve hours than most people can in eight."

An employee of the Toledo, Oregon, mill, Georgia-Pacific's first paper mill, uses a stick to check the tension of paper as it comes off the machine and is wound onto a roll. The paper will be converted into corrugated boxes. The Toledo mill, constructed in 1957, was the only pulp and paper mill ever built by G-P, which grew primarily by acquisition. When G-P bought a mill, it would bring it immediately into the company culture, a tradition that became known as "painting it blue," a reference to the color of the G-P logo.

and earned two master's degrees from Maine, in pulp and paper technology in 1966 and chemical engineering in 1967. That unique educational background proved to be an effective launching pad for the steep trajectory of his career. In many ways, going to Maine instead of Harvard was a maverick decision that proved later to be a masterstroke. From there, his career took him to the Weyerhaeuser Company for a decade, then on to 11 years at Mead Corporation, where he was senior vice president for forest products. At Mead, Correll was in a race for the top job that he ultimately lost. He reached the point where he disagreed with Mead's direction and called G-P's chairman and CEO, T. Marshall Hahn Jr., who offered him a job. Correll joined G-P in 1988. Five years later, he was G-P's chairman and chief executive officer.

His stroll on the beach that evening in 1997 was not born of satisfaction. Correll was troubled by the way major investors saw his company. The dollars that Georgia-Pacific earned weren't valued as highly as those earned by its rivals. That is, G-P could earn twice as much per share as competitors such as Weyerhaeuser or International Paper, yet its stock was valued about the same, instead of at twice as much. It was as if G-P's dollars didn't count as much. At one point, Correll recalls, he even seriously considered selling G-P but couldn't find a buyer that appreciated its value.

"We had to change not only Georgia-Pacific, but also the way the world thought of us," Correll explains. "Because no matter who made a comment about us, it was always followed by, 'They don't have

marketing skills and they boost sales by cutting prices.' That was not characteristic of our behavior, but that was characteristic of how the world saw us.

"I concluded that G-P was a good company, but that the market simply was not valuing what we were doing," he says. "We had tried everything — at least everything I knew how to do — to change that perception. Nothing worked."

The answer finally became clear as he heard his own advice coming back to him. He had often told others that insanity is "doing the same thing over and over and hoping the results will be different." In that moment, he realized that was just the approach G-P had been taking — for too long.

"My financial group had been coming to me with idea after idea," Correll says, "but nothing that looked right for G-P. Still, I heard their message: 'We have to do something different — *something different.*' And it finally occurred to me that resisting change was not the right thing for Georgia-Pacific to do.

"We had to shake things up."

Correll was about to make an enormous break with the past, but in doing so, he was also returning to the brash behavior that had made Georgia-Pacific one of the great growth stories in the history of American business.

For a half-century, Georgia-Pacific had been known as the maverick of the forest products industry. During the Great Depression, while competitors dropped like flies, the company's founder kept it alive by finding a European market for his hardwood lumber. Before the company turned 20, it began to

take the Pacific Northwest by storm from its home base in Augusta, Georgia. By the 1950s, as a rapidly growing public company, it was converting timber into plywood to fuel the homebuilding boom that followed World War II. G-P rapidly bought up vast tracts of Pacific Northwest timber with a revolutionary acquisition strategy. The company even moved its headquarters across America, to Portland, Oregon, to be closer to the green gold it was mining. As a growth story during its glory days, Georgia-Pacific's common stock "put on one of the most impressive showings of an exceptionally freewheeling period of the Big Board," *Forbes* magazine wrote in 1960. The stock rose from the equivalent of 2 3/4 in 1953 to 59 3/4 in 1960. "A starting investment of $1,000 would have grown to $20,000 in just seven years," *Forbes* said.

As Georgia-Pacific had bought up forests, it had financed them with one of the most creative strategies in the world of American business. It grew always by acquisition, buying dozens of companies and converting them overnight to G-P's decentralized culture, under which a manager had the freedom to run his operations as he saw fit — as long as he got the results the company expected. Along with that freedom came absolute responsibility. When goals weren't met, heads rolled like logs. The men who ran G-P were as tough as the lumberjacks who worked in the forests, although they always dressed to the nines.

Led by only five strong-willed chairmen across the 75 years of its history, the company showed a remarkable willingness to change. It virtually invented a new industry in the 1960s when it conducted secret experiments to make plywood from Southern pine. This effort generated a growth spurt so extraordinary that it brought down the full wrath of the federal government. After a quarter-century out West, Georgia-Pacific moved back to the South, to the then-troubled environs of downtown Atlanta, which it helped revitalize. Even into the 1990s, G-P was viewed as a maverick, as it acquired the Great Northern Nekoosa Corporation in the industry's first hostile takeover.

It was against this background — of a company that had boldly accumulated more than six million acres of timber — that Pete Correll just as boldly decided that Georgia-Pacific needed to sell its trees.

"That day on the beach, I realized that if the company was going to change, the change had to be dramatic," Correll says. "Of course, the most dramatic thing you can do as a forest products company is sell your trees. It had never been done. People have sold their companies, but no forest products company had ever sold its trees. Pulp and paper companies have sold their trees, but never before has the largest building products company in the world sold all its trees."

The decision sent shock waves through the company's old guard and the investment community. "I don't think that it's a good idea to get rid of the timber," said one of Correll's predecessors as chairman, Robert E. Flowerree, when he heard the news. "Timber is the main part of the company. All these plants are just a way of converting the timber into money."

Even Correll admitted his decision felt like defying

a basic, almost religious, belief. "I was raised believing that forest products companies had to own trees," he says. "I worked for Weyerhaeuser, and they define themselves as a tree-growing company. Selling the timberlands was a very, very difficult decision for me. But once I made the decision that we don't need trees, it freed me up mentally to look at everything. Because if trees weren't sacred, then nothing was sacred."

Correll's decision to sell the trees would ultimately move Georgia-Pacific out of the forests and deeper into the tissue industry, where he believed the company could avoid some of the whipsawing cycles that had buffeted both the building products and pulp and paper segments of G-P. As an example of the wild cyclical swings in the industry, Georgia-Pacific's building products segment posted a record operating profit of $1.2 billion for 1999. When that boom ended quickly and drastically, operating profits plummeted by more than two-thirds to $377 million the next year, followed by a loss in early 2001.

Georgia-Pacific was turning away from the vulnerability created by the macho philosophy of its past, best explained by Correll's chief confidante and close personal friend, the late Clint Kennedy, G-P's executive vice president of pulp and paper: "Run every ton you can run. Faster is bigger; bigger is better. That was the true culture of our industry — not just G-P, the whole industry."

As a result, Kennedy said, "the analysts think we're an industry of C students who never figured out the basic economics of running the business. We just cut down trees."

Whenever times were good, for instance, the industry invested in more capacity — not just one or two mammoth new paper machines, but 10 more. Then the industry would be faced with massive over-supply and plunging prices. After enormous capacity additions in the late 1980s, Georgia-Pacific began to wise up and develop the financial discipline not to continue pouring money back into new capacity. "We would generate so much cash we didn't know what to do with it," Kennedy said. "We've finally learned that you give it back to the shareholders if you can't come up with good projects."

The only place Georgia-Pacific could go, Correll reasoned, was closer to the consumer, shifting from a business portfolio dominated by such commodity-based forest products as market pulp and lumber to a mix of products dominated by higher-margin, less-cyclical consumer tissue products.

Selling G-P's timber holdings was the first of many exciting steps Correll would take at the turn of the twenty-first century to lead G-P in this direction. In 1997, to smooth the transition, G-P created a separate operating unit under the G-P umbrella, The Timber Company, and issued to shareholders a separate tracking stock that would be tied to the results of G-P's timber business. Correll believed that G-P could buy wood more cheaply if it didn't have to own it and that The Timber Company could sell it for more if they didn't have to transfer it within the company. Both notions proved true.

In 1999, G-P proceeded to make two major acquisitions that moved it closer to the end consumer.

The Timber Company's stock began trading on December 17, 1997, after it was formed as a separate operating company with six million acres of timber. Pete Correll and Don Glass, president and CEO of The Timber Company, wave from the New York Stock Exchange after ringing the bell to open the day's trading. Each person attending the celebratory breakfast that day received a commemorative medal, inset. Four years later, The Timber Company merged with Plum Creek Timber Company, Inc., a Seattle-based real estate investment trust, in a $4 billion transaction.

G-P acquired Unisource Worldwide Inc., a paper supplies and distribution business, for $1.5 billion. Analysts howled, and the stock plunged. But Correll and Lee Thomas, a G-P executive vice president and former head of the Environmental Protection Agency, stuck by their guns and insisted the acquisition would prove to be an excellent addition to the company. Georgia-Pacific also acquired Wisconsin Tissue, a move that vastly increased Georgia-Pacific's capacity in away-from-home tissue — the bathroom tissue and towels used in hotels and institutions.

By the summer of 2000, the timber business was ready to be spun off. G-P agreed for The Timber Company to merge with Plum Creek Timber Company, Inc., a real estate investment trust, in a $4 billion transaction. That same summer, G-P acquired the exclusive license to manufacture and market the Xerox brand of commodity multipurpose papers sold in the United States and Canada. The headlines that these deals might have generated were blasted off the front pages by an acquisition that would spell the future of G-P.

On July 17, 2000, Correll announced G-P would acquire Fort James Corporation for approximately $11 billion and become the world's biggest tissue maker. Fort James, the struggling combined company that resulted from the merger of Fort Howard Corporation and James River Corporation, had such

Pete Correll hosted a company-wide television broadcast in 1999 welcoming the employees of Unisource Worldwide, Inc., the nation's largest distributor of paper products, packaging and janitorial supplies, which G-P acquired for $1.5 billion. Analysts criticized the move, but Correll was confident the acquisition was an excellent addition to the G-P family.

On November 27, 2000, Georgia-Pacific completed the acquisition of Fort James Corporation and became the leading global producer of tissue products. The $11 billion transaction was a key part of Pete Correll's strategy for the transformation of G-P. On the day the deal closed, Correll flew to the former Fort James facility at Green Bay, Wisconsin, to greet the new employees, right. On the facing page, with Lee M. Thomas, executive vice president of consumer products, Correll smiles as they answer questions from new G-P employees against a backdrop of brands manufactured in Green Bay. Correll had hired Thomas in 1993 to head G-P's ambitious environmental program. Later, Correll said, "I stumbled onto one of the most talented executives I've ever met in my life." Thomas was Correll's right-hand man during the Fort James transaction.

strong brands as Brawny, Quilted Northern, Dixie, Mardi Gras and Vanity Fair. Fort James was the ideal acquisition candidate.

It was an opportunity G-P jumped on with relish, but it would force the divestiture of the Wisconsin Tissue assets to avoid antitrust problems. "The world was asking 'If you knew you were going to buy Fort James, why would you buy Wisconsin Tissue?'" Correll says. "Well, the answer, of course, is that in 1999 we had no idea we could buy Fort James."

Correll explained to a CNBC reporter on the morning of the announcement, "It's a big step in the transformation of Georgia-Pacific from a commodity-based company to a company that has brands and deals more directly with the consumer." Indeed, Georgia-Pacific was raking in major brand names — Dixie cups, Brawny and Xerox were among the most recognizable brands in America, and Quilted Northern was one of a very few 100-year-old brands in the country. And G-P was now selling through mass retailing customers, such as Wal-Mart, Kmart, Costco, Target, The Home Depot, Lowe's and Office Max.

A few hours after announcing the merger to the press, Correll, wearing a splendid, double-breasted

light brown suit, took to the stage in G-P headquarters in front of an auditorium full of employees, as employees elsewhere throughout the country watched via the company's business television satellite network. He opened with his characteristic good humor: "We like to use these sessions to clear up rumors. I got an e-mail from somebody that says, 'Is there any truth to the rumor that Georgia-Pacific is considering an acquisition of Fort James?'

"Yes, that's true," Correll said, as the room filled with laughter.

"This is a big day for our company," he continued. "This is a transforming acquisition that changes the way our company is viewed." He pointed out that Chief Financial Officer Danny W. Huff had been pounding on the importance of telling the world what G-P would be when it grows up.

"And now we've told the world," Correll said. "We have built this company being focused on raw materials and commodity products. What this is about is an effort to move us from that end of the value chain where we know the returns are low. Unisource did that. Wisconsin Tissue did that. The Xerox brand acquisition did that. And this does it in a big way. We know how to run facilities. We've got to position ourselves so we get paid for the products we make and the services we provide. That's what this move can do."

After the Fort James announcement, Rich Good, director of Georgia-Pacific's investor relations, took the market's temperature. "They think it's a good idea, because clearly this industry was in bad shape. It's an

industry that's fundamentally flawed. The forest products industry in general and the paper side of it in particular require way too much capital, and there's no return on that capital," Good explains.

In fact, Huff likes to point out that capital investments in the company's traditional businesses immediately depreciate. Running pulp and paper, for instance, means putting cash back into a segment of the industry that may or may not be growing. "Every now and then, you have to put a new boiler in a plant, and when you do that over time, you're destroying value. Because every time you put in a dollar, it's immediately worth 50 cents."

Even with the challenges inherent in the Fort James deal, Correll and his team felt they were on the right path as they headed into the new century. "The industry per se has been abysmal," says Huff. "The returns have been terrible and continue to be. A lot of people are still doing the same thing, and it's amazing to watch. On the other hand, we've always had the reputation of being the rogue of the group. I think that's good. I'm proud to be part of a company trying to do something different."

Correll's decision shook the very foundation of Georgia-Pacific and yet remained true to the character that had borne the company forward for 75 years. To understand the significance of Correll's revolution, it is important to understand the vision and the courage of the man who started it all, the man whose daughter still recalls the outraged reactions of the great timber barons of the Pacific Northwest, who once demanded to know, "Who is this upstart Owen Cheatham?"

A corporate display represents "Who We Are." The cross-section of Georgia-Pacific's diverse employees and widely ranging occupations includes representatives from the Unisource paper distribution business to timber and land management, information technology, mill manufacturing, research and development, communications and building products distribution. From a one-time male bastion, Georgia-Pacific evolved in the 1980s and 1990s into a more inclusive workforce, offering opportunities to men and women of all races and beliefs.

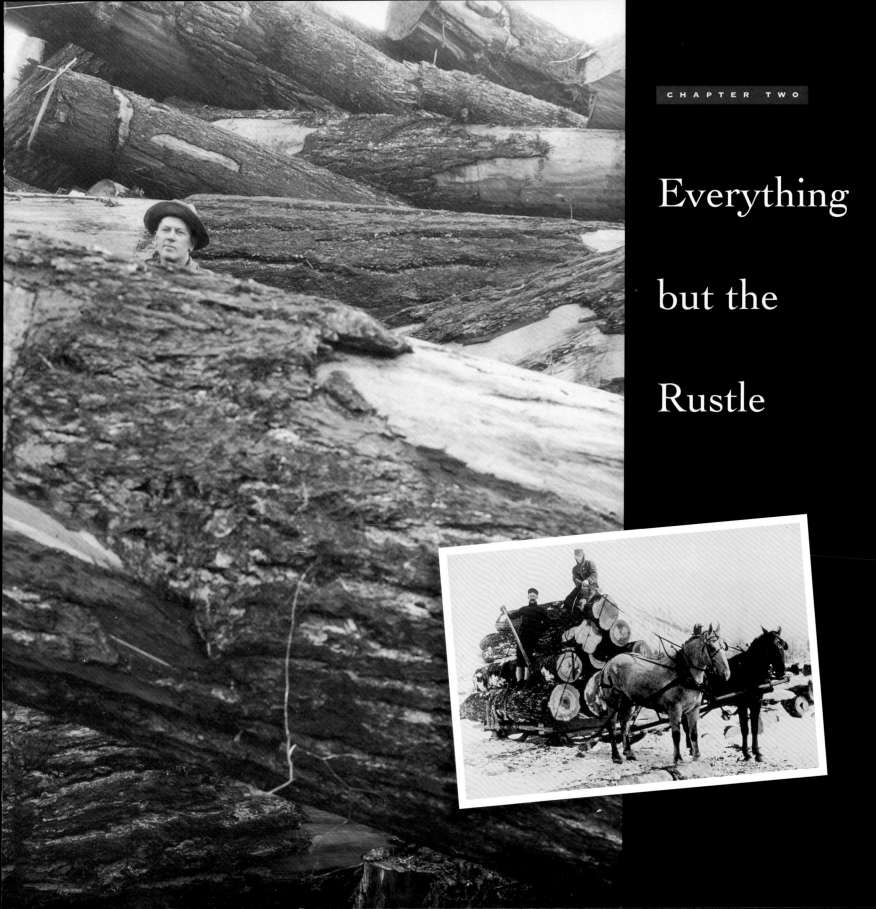

CHAPTER TWO

Everything

but the

Rustle

L ike Pete Correll, Owen R. Cheatham was a Southerner who lost his father at an early age. Cheatham's father, Walter, was a Virginia farmer and entrepreneur struck down by failing health. He lost his coal business and was forced to move his family to a farm in Concord, Virginia, owned by his wife's father, Sam Franklin, a descendant of Benjamin Franklin. Walter Cheatham died when most of his eight children were young.

As a boy growing up on a farm in rural Virginia, Owen R. Cheatham dreamed about becoming a woodsman. After completing his high school education at Hargrave Military Academy, where the portrait above right was taken, Cheatham entered the timber business against his grandfather's advice and formed the company that would become Georgia-Pacific.

Sam Franklin, a veteran of General Robert E. Lee's Army of Northern Virginia, was at Appomattox when Lee surrendered to Union General Ulysses S. Grant on April 2, 1865. On that day, many Confederate veterans began a long trek home that took some of them months. Franklin, on the other hand, "was home for lunch — Appomattox is about 11 miles from Concord," says Walter B. Cheatham II, Owen Cheatham's nephew and the last Cheatham to work for Georgia-Pacific. "My great-grandfather Franklin was probably the greatest influence on all the kids."

Owen, born in 1903, was the oldest boy in a family with four sons and four daughters. His younger brothers were Julian and Beverly, who later joined him at Georgia-Pacific, and William Henry, who stayed in Lynchburg, Virginia, where he owned a funeral home. Cheatham received his early religious training at the New Concord Presbyterian Church, where he acquired the faith and conservative ideals that guided him throughout his life.

At the end of his career, Owen looked back and recalled for G-P's internal magazine, *Growth*, his early dreams on his grandfather's farm:

"Small boys and trees are natural companions. Lying in the shade of a great old tree on a summer afternoon is an ideal place to dream dreams. And I dreamed them. I dreamed of being a woodsman. Timber was big business, but my otherwise wise grandfather counseled me: 'Stay out of the timber business. In 20 years, all of the timber will be cut down.' This is perhaps the one piece of Sam Franklin's advice I didn't take."

Because there was no public high school near the Franklin farm at the time, the family sacrificed to scrape together the money necessary to pay Owen's tuition to the private Hargrave Military Academy, a preparatory school in nearby Lynchburg.

Hargrave was the end of Owen Cheatham's formal education. He graduated and went into the world of business with an ambition to savor the finer things in life, an uncanny ability to learn by observing others and a world-class talent for selling. He would later be described by Portland, Oregon, newspaper reporter Anthony Bianco as "a soft-spoken, stylish charmer with the guts of a bandit."

The young Cheatham immediately tried to get a job with W. M. Ritter Lumber Company, which was widely viewed as the best company in the hardwood lumber business at the time. He was rebuffed and went into the railroad business for several years. But he would return to acquire W. M. Ritter nearly 40 years later.

Cheatham was hired in 1923 by his brother-in-law, William Dolan, who owned the Dolan Lumber Company in Lynchburg. Dolan asked Cheatham to build a hardwood division to complement his pine lumber business. For the next three years, Cheatham traveled the East Coast, learning the hardwood lumber business and polishing his natural gift for selling. In 1926, he moved to Augusta, Georgia, to manage one of Dolan's yards, with an eye toward starting his own business.

A salesman of extraordinary ability, Cheatham developed into a worldly sophisticate by observing the methods of successful people. He became a fastidious dresser with a taste for the finer things in life.

The young Cheatham immediately tried to get a job with W. M. Ritter Lumber Company, which was widely viewed as the best company in the hardwood lumber business at the time. He was rebuffed and went into the railroad business for several years. But he would return to acquire W. M. Ritter nearly 40 years later.

With $6,000 of his own and $6,000 borrowed, Cheatham purchased a wholesale lumberyard near Augusta in 1927, incorporated the business as the Georgia Hardwood Lumber Company and moved into its first "headquarters," above. Both deposits are recorded in the company's first bankbook, right, with Citizens & Southern Bank, where Cheatham met Mills B. Lane, a key financier of the company's growth.

HIS OWN COMPANY

Cheatham quickly became a social fixture in the golf-obsessed home of the Augusta National Golf Club, which hosts the Masters Tournament each year. There, he became an avid golfer and married Celeste Wickliffe, a high school physical education teacher.

In 1927, Cheatham purchased a wholesale lumberyard for $12,000. He had only $6,000 of his own money to invest, but he quickly displayed his genius for creative financing. He went home to Lynchburg and raised $3,000 each from J. Hunt Hargrave, chairman of the board of Hargrave Military

Academy, and J. Hurt Whitehead, president of Planters Bank in Chatham, Virginia.

On September 22, 1927, Cheatham incorporated the Georgia Hardwood Lumber Company. He issued 120 shares of common stock: 60 for himself and 30 each to Hargrave and Whitehead.

When he bought the lumberyard, he walked out to meet the yard hands and won them over immediately by sharing his ambitious plan to dramatically increase the size of the business.

Business at first was brisk for Cheatham, who was taking advantage of the pent-up demand for home construction that followed the end of World War I. But the company was barely two years old when the stock market crashed in October 1929. Cheatham survived the Great Depression by keeping his inventories low. He sold the lumber he purchased from sawmills as fast as he could, sometimes selling an order before he bought the lumber. He soon developed an eye for international business. By 1932, his business had grown to the point where he felt comfortable hiring another salesman, Eugene Howerdd, who introduced him to the export market. Cheatham took a tour of Europe that

year and quickly developed an export business in hardwood, taking orders in Belgium, France, Germany, Holland and Spain.

"I took a trip to Europe and discovered that other countries were coming out of the Depression much earlier than we were," Cheatham wrote. "Our little company in Augusta could buy wood at depressed prices here at home, ship it abroad and sell it for increased prices on the other side."

In 1932, he met in New York City with Sir Isaac Wolfson of the Great Universal Stores, a British chain described as the Sears Roebuck of Europe. "He asked to see me at the old Waldorf in New York and, after three days, gave me the largest single order in lumber industry history — one thousand carloads," Cheatham wrote. "Thereafter, Wolfson purchased many thousand other carloads of our product."

Success in Europe led to expansion at home. By 1934, Georgia Hardwood Lumber Co. was beginning to prosper. As his roadside lumberyard became a lumber company, Cheatham began his movement into finer quarters. As soon as practical, he opened a headquarters office on the 16th floor of the Southern Finance Building in Augusta for himself and the five employees who made up the office staff. The company had begun a growth spurt that would continue for decades to come.

In the new surroundings, Cheatham shared the philosophical observations that helped transform him from a Virginia farm boy into an international sophisticate. He urged his employees to improve themselves through self-criticism and by observing

Georgia Hardwood survived the Depression by keeping inventories and expenses low and by exporting hardwood lumber to Europe. In 1934, Georgia Hardwood moved uptown to an office on the 16th floor of the Southern Finance Building in Augusta, above. At the time, Cheatham had only five employees, but his company's great growth spurt had begun.

the methods of successful people. A fastidious dresser, Cheatham demanded that his employees dress neatly at all times. Men who worked in the office were required to wear suits or sports jackets, even on coffee breaks. He demanded clean desks, which had to remain in perfect alignment. He would not allow adding machine tape to run over the side of the desk and touch the floor.

Cheatham had taken on a more corporate air since his speech to lumberyard workers in 1927. In the office, his written communications to employees were formal, philosophical and florid: "Lumber is a necessity, and we help to supply it to nearly all parts of the world. Wood is beautiful, lovely to look at, to live with and to touch. From each tree nature could tell a different story. Wood was made to be used, and nature renews it, year after year. There will always be adequate timber for all reasonable needs."

Even the coffee breaks in Augusta approached the formality of high tea, recalls Marion Talmadge, who joined the company in the 1940s and rose to the position of treasurer. However, the beverage of choice in Georgia at the time tended to be Coca-Cola rather than tea.

"At 10:30 a.m., a man named Woody Johnson would serve coffee in china cups, poured from a silver pitcher," Talmadge says. "Then at 3:30 in the afternoon, we'd have a Coca-Cola."

One of Cheatham's most important contacts in the social hothouse of tiny Augusta was Mills B. Lane, who would rise to the presidency of Citizens & Southern Bank, which would become one of the key banks that make up Bank of America today. Lane built a reputation as an iconoclastic wild man in the staid world of banking, and he introduced Cheatham to key people in the national banking industry and served on

Uniform Domestic Straight Bill of Lading Adopted by Carriers in Official, Southern and Western Classification Territories, March

THIS MEMORANDUM is an acknowledgement that a Bill of Lading has been issued and is not the Original Bill of Lading, nor a copy or duplicate covering the property named herein, and is intended solely for filing or record.

GEORGIA RAILROAD

RECEIVED, subject to the classifications and tariffs in effect on the date of the receipt by the carrier of the in the Original Bill of Lading.

at **Augusta, Ga.**   **Sept. 1, 1927.**

from **Georgia Hardwood Lumber Company,**

Consigned to **Schofield Lance Company,**

Destination **Hershey**   State of **Pa.**   County of

Route **Via A.C.L.**

Reading R.R. Delivery.   Car Initial **Ga.**   Car No.

No Packages	DESCRIPTION OF ARTICLES, SPECIAL MARKS AND EXCEPTIONS	*WEIGHT (Subject to Correction)	CLASS OR RATE	CHECK COLUMN	
1	C/L Dry Poplar Lumber				
	Milled in transit from Culverton, Ga. Car Ga. 18151 - Pro 6575 - 8/29/27 - 9431 ft Car NC&StL 15382 " 6576 - 8/29/27 - 8514 ft 17945 Total feet in this car 17445 ft.				

Lathe Apron

Georgia Hardwood's board of directors and later on Georgia–Pacific's board of directors.

"Mills Lane was a maverick, too," Talmadge recalls. "He did all kinds of funny things like ride a motor scooter through the bank. He would bring in animals. He was always laughing, greeting his customers. Everything was wonderful with Mills Lane. He was very different from Mr. Cheatham, who was much more conservative, but they became very good friends."

Perhaps the most important step Cheatham took in 1934 was a personnel move. He hired a new bookkeeper, Robert B. Pamplin, who had roomed with Owen's younger brother Julian at Virginia Polytechnic Institute. While Julian took a job with Western Union, Pamplin had gone on to Northwestern University to study finance.

Pamplin was a perfect fit. Owen Cheatham and Eugene Howerdd were gregarious salesmen. Pamplin, on the other hand, was an analytical, precise and blunt accountant who was relentlessly competitive. He added a very necessary component to the growing company's top ranks. Pamplin was the accounting genius who would find ways

As the company opened lumberyards in communities such as Winona, Mississippi, above, Cheatham became more of a promoter. He made sure that the name "Georgia Hardwood Lumber Company" was stamped in red on the end of each board of its premium yellow pine, which was some of the best wood on the market. Wood veneer rolls off a lathe, opposite, at a Georgia Hardwood mill.

Julian Cheatham, above, was Owen's younger brother. He joined Georgia Hardwood in 1937, but before that, he scouted talent for his brother, including Robert B. Pamplin, Julian's college roommate from Virginia Polytechnic Institute. Owen hired Pamplin in 1934. Together, they would form one of the great executive teams of the twentieth century, opposite. Pamplin, who later became chairman and CEO, was a blunt accountant with an astonishing gift for figuring out how to finance all of Owen Cheatham's dreams. Both men were rock-ribbed conservatives, but were willing to take enormous risks.

to fund all of Owen Cheatham's dreams. Cheatham and Pamplin produced one of the most creative and productive executive teams of the American century.

"Bob Pamplin's brilliance was in figures, mathematical things," recalls Talmadge. "Mr. Cheatham was a salesman. They worked in combination very well. Owen would come up with an idea and then tell Bob to figure out how we should do it."

Like Cheatham, Pamplin was raised on a Virginia farm. He spent his youth raising and selling farm produce. He was diligent, ambitious and deeply religious. In Augusta, he met and married Katherine Reese.

Pamplin was far more than an accountant from the start, because his crisp linear thinking was a perfect fit with Cheatham's overwhelming desire for order. He was an integral part of the company's operations, a visionary thinker who would become not only Cheatham's right-hand man, but also a leader who would not hesitate to argue a point with the company founder. What made Cheatham and Pamplin such an unusual pair was that they were rock-ribbed conservatives in thought, word and deed, yet both were willing to take enormous risks — once Pamplin had worked the numbers.

"In the early days of the company, Bob Pamplin had great influence because he knew the proper accounting methods, and that was exactly what Owen needed," Julian Cheatham said in *Growth* in 1976. "He used to get the mail at the post office, open it and read it. He knew everything that was going on."

In 1937, Julian Cheatham joined his brother and his friend Pamplin at Georgia Hardwood. He moved

to Augusta to handle hardwood sales. Julian had a keen eye for personnel and was considered a more level-headed judge of talent than Owen, who occasionally fell for a glib story. Julian had an uncanny knack for finding the right people for Owen to hire. He worked almost like a talent scout, yet he also held numerous high-level positions in the company.

"His mother always said that Owen was the brains of the family and Julian was the heart," says Julian's widow, Alyce Cheatham. Their roles set Owen up as the officer in charge, while Julian was the loyal sergeant who always took care to watch out for the younger siblings. "According to Mrs. Cheatham, whenever they went somewhere, Julian was the one who would insure everybody came home when they were supposed to," Alyce says.

Julian and Alyce met through her job at Augusta National Golf Club, where she worked for the legendary golfer Bobby Jones. "It was a gorgeous job," she recalls. "They kept telling me, 'we have only one bachelor as a member, so we're going to save him for you. It was Julian.'"

By 1938, Georgia Hardwood was operating five sawmills in the South. As the nation entered the Second World War, the buildup of war matériel increased the demand for lumber to build barracks and other buildings. Between 1941 and 1945, Georgia Hardwood acquired mills and lumberyards throughout the Carolinas, Alabama and Mississippi.

The war also provided a boom in hardwood lumber sales to the British, who lacked the timber resources of America and desperately needed the

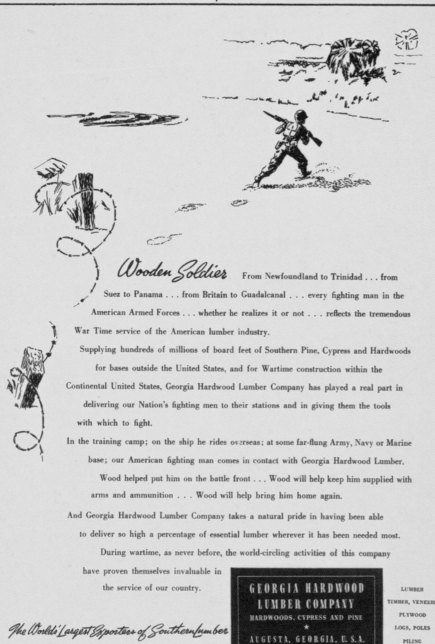

Wooden Soldier From Newfoundland to Trinidad . . . from Suez to Panama . . . from Britain to Guadalcanal . . . every fighting man in the American Armed Forces . . . whether he realizes it or not . . . reflects the tremendous War Time service of the American lumber industry.

Supplying hundreds of millions of board feet of Southern Pine, Cypress and Hardwoods for bases outside the United States, and for Wartime construction within the Continental United States, Georgia Hardwood Lumber Company has played a real part in delivering our Nation's fighting men to their stations and in giving them the tools with which to fight.

In the training camp; on the ship he rides overseas; at some far-flung Army, Navy or Marine base; our American fighting man comes in contact with Georgia Hardwood Lumber. Wood helped put him on the battle front . . . Wood will help keep him supplied with arms and ammunition . . . Wood will help bring him home again.

And Georgia Hardwood Lumber Company takes a natural pride in having been able to deliver so high a percentage of essential lumber wherever it has been needed most. During wartime, as never before, the world-circling activities of this company have proven themselves invaluable in the service of our country.

The World's Largest Exporters of Southern Lumber

GEORGIA HARDWOOD LUMBER COMPANY
HARDWOODS, CYPRESS AND PINE
★
AUGUSTA, GEORGIA, U.S.A.

LUMBER
TIMBER, VENEERS
PLYWOOD
LOGS, POLES
PILING

LITHOGRAPHED IN U.S.A.

wood to build for the war effort as well as to repair damage from German bombs.

Eugene Howerdd found a way for Georgia Hardwood to become a supplier for the U.S. Army Corps of Engineers. Creating an enterprise called Georgia Distributing Yards (GDY), Howerdd proposed stockpiling lumber marked for the Corps of Engineers at supply depots set up in the yards of the Lumbermens Merchandising Corporation (LMC) of Philadelphia, a group buying organization made up of independent lumbermen.

LMC was organized as a stroke of genius by James Buckley, a suave Northeasterner who had graduated from the University of Pennsylvania's Wharton School of Finance and Commerce and who would become one of Owen Cheatham's most trusted associates. GDY supplied about 80 million feet of lumber for the war effort and was awarded the Army/Navy "E" Award for its role in supplying lumber to U.S. forces overseas.

THE WAY WEST

Owen Cheatham convinced Buckley, who had numerous industry contacts, to join Georgia Hardwood in October 1943 to head its business in the East out of New York City. He proved to be an enormously important and versatile hire, because he had just as many contacts in the Pacific Northwest. He had gotten to know several of the larger manufacturing firms in the Northwest while purchasing lumber and plywood for LMC. In fact, he had formed whiskey-drinking friendships with a number of important timbermen. Buckley persuaded Cheatham to include in his company's product mix plywood and lumber made of Douglas fir from the Northwest.

Cheatham quickly saw the potential of plywood. "We had found that plywood would bring three times the return of lumber, and we knew that vast markets for plywood were waiting for cultivation," Cheatham wrote. He knew that demand for housing would skyrocket when the war ended, and he wanted Georgia Hardwood to be manufacturing plywood when that construction boom began.

The only place for the plywood business at the time was the Northwest, where lush forests of Douglas fir in western Oregon and Washington constituted 40 percent of the saw timber in the United States and produced two-thirds of the nation's plywood. Buckley introduced Cheatham to the hard-edged lumbermen of the Northwest in 1947 at a dinner he had hosted annually in Portland.

Cheatham was staggered by the scale of operations in the Northwest, particularly at some of the large mills at C. D. Johnson Lumber Co. and Bloedel-Donovan Lumber Mills, which turned out 500,000 feet or more of lumber each day. He was particularly impressed with the plywood operations, where he saw eight- to ten-foot peeler logs of Douglas fir unrolled on a lathe down to a 12-inch core, producing a long sheet of veneer that

was cut into pieces and glued into a four-by-eight-foot panel of sandwiched layers. The finished product was, pound for pound, stronger than steel.

Owen Cheatham was determined to acquire as much plywood capacity as possible. He just had to find a way to pay for it.

Georgia Hardwood entered the plywood business

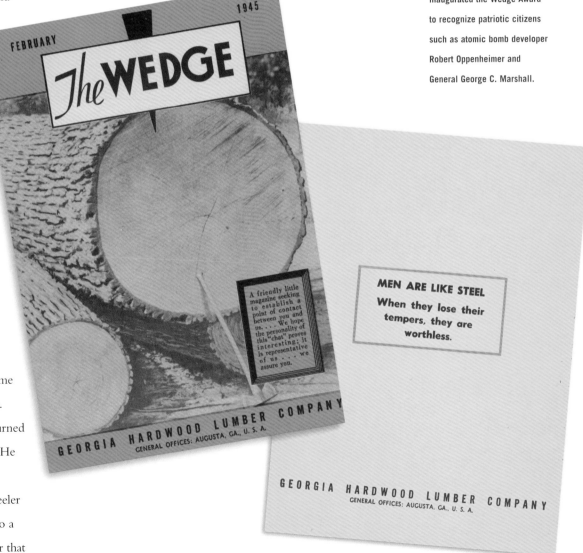

Business boomed as Georgia Hardwood supplied lumber for the U.S. Army. In 1943, Cheatham hired James Buckley, who eventually persuaded him to market Douglas fir plywood and lumber from the Pacific Northwest, where the rugged woodsmen known as "timber beasts" brought down mammoth redwoods with axes and saws in primeval forests such as this one in Fort Bragg, California, left.

The Northwest was the last frontier for the lumber industry, excluding Alaska. Lush forests of Douglas fir grew in the rainy climes of western Oregon and Washington. In just 100 years, the region had seen trappers and miners give way to lumbermen, who changed their ways little from 1900 to World War II, still wearing red hats and "tin" pants.

Cheatham was awed by the scale of the Northwestern lumber and logging operations. At left, old-fashioned loggers maintain their balance on a water-born log in Oregon, while a wigwam burner behind them burns wood chips and bark as waste, literally sending the wood up in smoke. Today, such byproducts are converted into power to run plants and emissions have been diminished drastically.

Above, a horse-drawn sled with enormous wheels pulls logs to mills. In this vast region, Cheatham saw the potential for the postwar boom in housing, which would demand plywood.

in 1947 with the purchase of Bellingham Plywood Company, a cooperative organized in 1941 by a group of businessmen, for the then-staggering amount of $1,113,248. Cheatham had carefully prepared for this moment by establishing his company's reputation in the financial community. He paid for the purchase by taking his stock public in 1947, on the advice of Clifford Roberts, a partner in the New York investment firm of Reynolds & Company, who happened to be chairman of the board of the Augusta National Golf Club. The company sold 100,000 shares of common stock at $8.20 per share, initially netting $700,000. Additional shares of preferred and common stock were sold to raise the purchase price.

With the purchase of Bellingham Plywood, the company had grown to 750 employees and its annual sales totaled $24 million.

The next year, 1948, the company changed its name from Georgia Hardwood Lumber Company to Georgia-Pacific Plywood and Lumber Company. That same year, Cheatham acquired from Weyerhaeuser Company a controlling interest in Washington Veneer, which owned two plywood mills at Olympia and a 60 percent interest in Springfield Plywood Company of Springfield, Oregon.

To make the deal work, Cheatham needed a banker with deep pockets. Mills Lane introduced him to officials at Bank of America in San Francisco. There, Cheatham met with the bank's then-vice president of finance, Fred Ferroggiaro, who was so impressed that he would later describe Cheatham as

Cheatham knew the postwar building boom would demand vast amounts of plywood. In 1947, he paid $1.1 million for the Bellingham Plywood Company in Bellingham, Washington, above. Workers at Bellingham stack pieces of layered wood covered with glue into the press that will create sheets of plywood, left. Cheatham decided to take his company public, selling 100,000 shares of common stock at $8.20 per share to help finance the purchase of Bellingham.

Cheatham continued buying his way into the plywood business. In 1948, he paid $3.5 million for controlling interests in Washington Veneer at Olympia, Washington, and Springfield Plywood Company in Springfield, Oregon, above. These two plants combined with the burgeoning Bellingham operation, opposite, to make Georgia Hardwood a leading plywood producer in the country and second to U.S. Plywood in sales. The company changed its name to Georgia-Pacific Plywood & Lumber Company that same year.

"one of the greatest and brightest people living."

Ferroggiaro, who started as a messenger boy and eventually worked his way up to chairman of the board, apparently saw something of himself in Owen Cheatham. He granted the loan and would later serve on Georgia-Pacific's board of directors. Bank of America would become the lead bank for the company, which also relied heavily on longer-term loans from the Metropolitan Life Insurance Company and The Prudential Insurance Company. Cheatham pooled the Bank of America loan with additional financing through the sale of stock and paid $3.5 million for the interests in Washington Veneer and Springfield Plywood.

In 1949, the company got into the plywood business back home as well, buying a hardwood plywood plant that had just been built in Savannah, Georgia, by owners who decided not to operate it because they were losing money.

"I arranged to meet their key man at the Stork Club in New York," Cheatham wrote. "I asked him right away how much he wanted for the plant. He said '$2.2 million.' I said that we would give $300,000 — no more. He said immediately that we had bought the cheapest plywood plant in existence."

With three major acquisitions in three years, Owen Cheatham had planted a large footprint in the U.S. plywood industry. Georgia-Pacific was already the leading plywood producer and ranked second to U.S. Plywood in sales, but G-P quickly encountered the culture clash and organizational challenge of selling relatively stable plywood through a sales force used to

the volatility of the lumber business. Cheatham brought in Stewart White from the Pacific Mutual Door Company to manage G-P's warehouse system and fix the problem.

A CHANGE OF HEART

Cheatham proclaimed in the late 1940s that he was not interested in owning vast tracts of forests. The company was not long removed from the Depression, when many lumber companies that owned timberland were driven into bankruptcy, unable to pay taxes on the land. Moreover, his grandfather's advice still rung in his ears: how much longer would the North American timberlands last? Cheatham reconfirmed this position in Georgia-Pacific's 1948 annual report, writing, "It is not the policy of the company to hold extremely large timber tracts with the attendant high carrying costs and risks." But Cheatham would soon change his mind.

On January 27, 1949, less than two years after it first took its stock public, Georgia-Pacific stock was listed on the New York Stock Exchange. Later that year, a recession hit the industry and sent the price of plywood crashing. Between October 1948 and June 1949, the price of ¼-inch plywood dropped from a high of $110 per thousand square feet to a low of $36. It would take nearly 20 years for the price to climb back to $100. Competition and better utilization of wood would keep the price low.

The recession of 1949, rather than reinforcing the familiar fears of owning timberlands, showed

On January 27, 1949, less than two years after Georgia-Pacific went public, its stock was listed on the New York Stock Exchange.

Cheatham the difficulties facing Georgia-Pacific —
now heavily invested in the plywood business — if it
did *not* own its own timberlands.

Cheatham's friend and board member Harvey
Fruehauf Sr., who he had met through the Augusta
National Golf Club, offered Cheatham some advice
on the subject. Harvey "Bud" Fruehauf Jr., who
succeeded his father on G-P's board, recalls the story
of the encounter on the golf course.

"Dad said, 'Owen, you've got to own your own
timber so you can control your raw material costs.'

"And Owen said, 'That's fine, Harvey, I'd like to
do that. But I don't have any money.'

"Dad said, 'Then you must borrow it.'

"'Yes,' Owen said, 'but that isn't easily done.'

"Dad said, 'No, of course not. But you go to the
New York bankers and investment bankers and work
this thing out. Your story is a good one, and it should
work.'"

Fruehauf's recommendation would set the stage
for a timberland-buying binge that would last a decade.

In 1950, Georgia-Pacific decided to acquire
C. D. Johnson Lumber Company, a family-owned
firm in Toledo, Oregon, that had purchased a spruce
mill from the government after World War I and also
owned its own timberlands. Brothers Dean and
Ernest Johnson flew to Chicago to meet with
Cheatham, Pamplin and Buckley to negotiate a deal.
The parties drafted an agreement for Georgia-Pacific
to acquire the company.

But tragedy struck. The brothers were killed on
their way home when their plane crashed in the hills

north of Oakland, California. A fast-moving G-P
lawyer retrieved a copy of the agreement from the
wreckage, but it was challenged by a major stock-
holder in C. D. Johnson, driving up the price.
Georgia-Pacific paid more than it had originally
planned — $16.8 million for 66,000 acres of heavily
cut timberlands and a sawmill.

G-P financed the purchase through a temporary
$12.6 million loan from Bank of America, plus
$1.2 million from the company treasury and
$3 million from the sale of stock. G-P later repaid
the Bank of America loan with loans of $4 million
each from Metropolitan Life and Prudential. The
remaining $4.6 million came from the sale of 250,000

Celebrating Georgia-Pacific's
first day listed on the New York
Stock Exchange, opposite,
were (left to right) Willard
Heinrich, Eugene Howerdd,
NYSE president Emil Schramm,
Owen Cheatham, S. Rexford
Black, James Buckley and an
unidentified guest. The sale of
stock helped Georgia-Pacific
buy the C. D. Johnson Lumber
Company of Toledo, Oregon,
above. Augusta-based
Georgia-Pacific would soon
have 60 percent of its assets
in the Northwest.

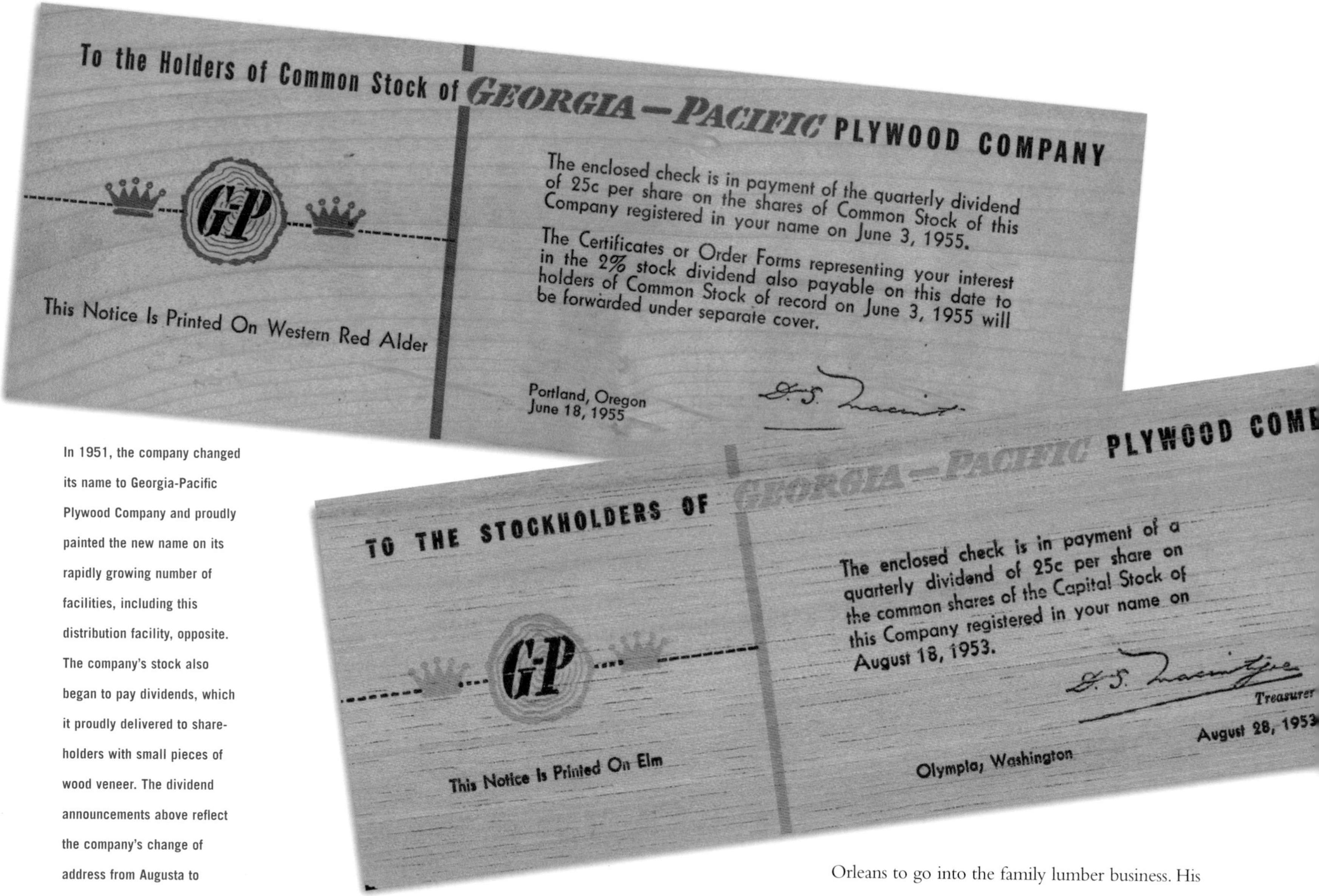

To the Holders of Common Stock of GEORGIA–PACIFIC PLYWOOD COMPANY

The enclosed check is in payment of the quarterly dividend of 25c per share on the shares of Common Stock of this Company registered in your name on June 3, 1955.

The Certificates or Order Forms representing your interest in the 2% stock dividend also payable on this date to holders of Common Stock of record on June 3, 1955 will be forwarded under separate cover.

This Notice Is Printed On Western Red Alder

Portland, Oregon
June 18, 1955

TO THE STOCKHOLDERS OF GEORGIA–PACIFIC PLYWOOD COMPANY

The enclosed check is in payment of a quarterly dividend of 25c per share on the common shares of the Capital Stock of this Company registered in your name on August 18, 1953.

This Notice Is Printed On Elm

Olympia, Washington

Treasurer
August 28, 1953

In 1951, the company changed its name to Georgia-Pacific Plywood Company and proudly painted the new name on its rapidly growing number of facilities, including this distribution facility, opposite. The company's stock also began to pay dividends, which it proudly delivered to shareholders with small pieces of wood veneer. The dividend announcements above reflect the company's change of address from Augusta to Olympia, Washington in 1953 and to Portland, Oregon, the following year.

shares of common stock and funds of C. D. Johnson. G-P closed the purchase of C. D. Johnson in 1951, the same year it changed its name to Georgia-Pacific Plywood Company.

Just days before the Johnsons perished in the plane crash, one of their brightest young employees had left the mill and moved back home to New Orleans to go into the family lumber business. His name was Robert E. Flowerree.

Flowerree had gone to C. D. Johnson to learn the nature of the highly cyclical lumber business and then had returned home to work for his grandfather, a Louisiana timber baron named Harry Hewes, who had a substantial interest in C. D. Johnson. "I remember my grandfather saying that the only time anyone ever made any money in the lumber business was

Robert E. Flowerree, above, joined Georgia-Pacific through its acquisition of C. D. Johnson. A Tulane University graduate, he had planned to go back home to join the family timber business in Louisiana, but Cheatham persuaded him to join G-P. Flowerree played a vital role in the integration of the company's resources and expansion into new uses for forest products. He later rose to the positions of chairman and CEO.

when San Francisco had an earthquake and a fire," Flowerree says. But Cheatham persuaded him to move back to Toledo and manage the mill for Georgia-Pacific.

A NEW HOME

As Georgia-Pacific shifted its focus to plywood, still dominated by the Douglas fir of the Northwest, Cheatham found his company had outgrown its Augusta roots. He moved some functions to New York City to be closer to the all-important financiers who were enabling the company's growth. In May 1949, Cheatham organized the company into Eastern, Southern, Midwestern and Western zones, each under a vice president, to handle the functions of selling, purchasing and manufacturing. The zones became formal divisions in 1950.

Pamplin, who was administrative vice president at the time, refused to go north, telling Cheatham the planned move was "the craziest thing I ever heard," he recalled later. Cheatham removed Pamplin from the board of directors and did not reinstate him until 1955. But Pamplin was not the only recalcitrant Southerner. Cheatham found it impossible to transfer employees from Augusta to New York.

Cheatham decided to keep an office and home in New York to stay close to his new financial contacts — not to mention the social whirl of Manhattan, where he kept a chauffeur-driven Rolls Royce — but he gave up on moving the company to New York. Instead, he commissioned a management study to determine the

benefit of moving the company headquarters west.

Georgia-Pacific now had 60 percent of its assets in the Northwest, 25 percent in the South and the rest in warehouses in the Midwest and East. The study recommended moving the company headquarters to Seattle, but Cheatham decided in 1953 to move the headquarters to Olympia, Washington, where the two Washington Veneer plants were located. The stay there was short-lived. Cheatham put Pamplin in charge of the new headquarters. Pamplin was not sure he wanted to stay in the West and also was not sure if employees would accept him in the role of running the company. He agreed to try the new role and the new location, but only for two years, and he kept open the option of returning to Augusta to start his own company. Eugene Howerdd took early retirement and stayed in Augusta.

Cheatham decided to bring in an outsider to replace Howerdd, but the new hire turned out to be oil to Pamplin's water. In the early 1950s, when General Dwight D. Eisenhower was President of the United States, it was fashionable for corporations to hire generals. Georgia-Pacific was no exception. Cheatham hired Major General Lewis Pick from the U.S. Army Corps of Engineers, who had supervised the building of the Ledo Road in the China-India-Burma Theater during World War II, known as "Pick's Pike."

As successful as he had been in the military, "General Pick didn't know much about the lumber business or the plywood business," Robert Flowerree recalls. "I think his biggest problem was that he didn't understand the sales role. He thought that you could go ahead and raise the price and everybody would pay it. But they didn't. They went to Weyerhaeuser or to somebody else. So he and the distribution people really had problems." Pick clashed with important G-P employees almost as soon as he arrived in Olympia.

When the general decided to go to church on his first Sunday in Olympia, Marion Talmadge and his wife were asked to take him. "We were designated to take the general to the Presbyterian Church in Olympia," Talmadge recalls. "We opened the door and he proceeded to the front row." Talmadge, a Southern gentleman, was shocked by the general's grand entrance, which drew the attention of everyone in the sanctuary. "I've never been so embarrassed in my life," he says.

Morale at the new headquarters began to plunge under Pick. "Owen had hired him, yet Owen wasn't there in Olympia to see what was going on," Talmadge recalls. "He was in New York." The conflict came to a head when Pamplin decided to leave the company and return to Augusta. His wife, Katherine, had already moved back, and he had had enough of General Pick. Cheatham finally stepped in.

"Owen said it was all a mistake with Pick and he would let him go if I stayed on," Pamplin later told *Willamette Week*. Pamplin drew up a contract, and Cheatham agreed to it.

Then G-P decided to move again.

"The trouble with Olympia was transportation," recalls Marion Talmadge. "You had to fly into Seattle and be picked up and taken to Olympia. And everything arrived to Olympia a day late. They decided the company headquarters had to be in a big place. That's when they decided to move to Portland." The company moved its headquarters from Olympia to Portland in 1954.

By the time Georgia-Pacific had moved its headquarters to the top floor of the Equitable Building in Portland, Oregon, Owen Cheatham had taken to heart Harvey Fruehauf's advice about owning timberland. Further cementing that decision, in 1953, the Federal Reserve Board amended its regulations to permit banks to lend money on forestlands. And in Georgia-Pacific's 1954 annual report, Cheatham officially reversed his earlier position, declaring: "Under the company's plan of operation, the long-term debt incurred in its timber acquisition program is self-liquidating, through the use of timber, and imposes no drain on the company's cash resources."

The acquisition of C. D. Johnson and its timberlands in Toledo, Oregon, was already proving this to be true. The timberlands were so heavily cut when G-P bought them that if cutting had continued at the C. D. Johnson rate, "there was only enough timber in the area to last another nine years," Cheatham wrote. "Toledo's economy was supposed to wither and die and Georgia-Pacific was rumored to be just the kind of fast-cutting outfit that would hasten the disaster."

At a time when military heroes were in high demand, Cheatham hired former Major General Lewis Pick, who didn't know much about the lumber or plywood businesses. Pick clashed with Pamplin, who nearly left the company. Cheatham chose Pamplin over Pick.

THE STYLE OF OWEN CHEATHAM

Celeste and Owen Cheatham became major social figures in Portland, New York and Palm Beach, Florida, where they owned a villa called "Tranquility" facing the Atlantic Ocean. In the photo opposite, Cheatham relaxes at Tranquility.

Owen Cheatham grew up on his grandfather's Maple Valley Farm reading the work of a distant forebear and dreaming of a career in timber. For Georgia-Pacific's 40th anniversary, Cheatham wrote in *Growth* that his grandfather was the great-great-grandnephew of Benjamin Franklin and "I became well acquainted with the practical philosophy of *Poor Richard's Almanac*."

Cheatham dispensed practical advice throughout his life to employees and family members, leaning on the conservative values he learned from his grandfather and the businessmen he admired on his way up. But he also generously dispensed stock to his relatives and — with his wife, Celeste — created a lifestyle worthy of Jay Gatsby, with mansions on both coasts and a lavish apartment in New York City.

His ambition burned hotter because his family was almost penniless as a child. "They were very poor. I mean, they didn't have a dime," says his daughter, Celeste Wickliffe Cheatham. "My father had a star to follow, and he just followed it."

Cheatham's reputation as a businessman flourished as his company grew. "Owen Cheatham is one of the few authentic geniuses in American industry today," a "well-known Wall Streeter" told *Forbes* in a June 15, 1960, cover story about Georgia-Pacific headlined, "The Amazing House that Owen Cheatham Built."

By that time, Cheatham, an ardent Republican, had become friends with President Dwight Eisenhower and Vice President Richard Nixon. *Forbes* estimated Cheatham's personal fortune at $20 million in the early 1960s.

But the Cheathams' social whirl had begun three decades earlier in Augusta, where Owen Cheatham met and married Celeste Wickliffe. Owen became a member of the Augusta National Golf Club, created by the great Georgia golfer Bobby Jones and home to the Masters Tournament.

He and Celeste bought a mansion surrounded by azaleas on Bransford Road in Augusta, They named it "Cheatwick" and began adding rooms as they had two

As they became more socially prominent, the Cheathams acquired the Dali Jewels, elaborate pieces of jewelry that resembled the surrealistic paintings of the artist Salvador Dali. The Owen Cheatham Foundation owned the jewels and sent them on tours to raise money for charities.

daughters, Celeste, also known as Wickie, and Mary Fenton, nicknamed Cynthia.

As Cheatham's company began growing and adding plywood facilities, he took a small apartment in New York City to be near the lenders that could fuel his company's growth. Then his daughter Celeste, diagnosed with scoliosis, was referred by the Mayo Clinic to a doctor in New York. "My mother came to New York and she fell in love with it," Celeste recalls. "We all fell in love with New York." The family eventually bought a large apartment at the River House in Manhattan, which became home.

"The apartment was quite large, with three or four bedrooms, plus servant quarters, and a beautiful library," recalls Alyce Cheatham, widow of Owen's brother Julian.

In New York, Owen Cheatham turned to Al DuPont, of the chemical family, to begin introducing him to social contacts after he took Georgia-Pacific public.

"Al DuPont introduced my parents to lots of people," Celeste says. "You know, when you first go to a city, it's hard to break in, especially New York. But they became Mr. and Mrs. New York. I'm not kidding. They really did." DuPont tutored the Cheathams on the opera, the theater and which nightclubs they should frequent.

"My mother was always running this ball and that ball and she was head of the Junior League. She loved it. And it was good for my Daddy. Oh, Mr. and Mrs. Owen Cheatham were really quite the team. They really were wonderful together."

Their parties were always black-tie affairs and drew such celebrities as the actor Charles Coburn and the actress Celeste Holme.

Cheatham made a splash for several years with his

"Wedge" Awards, named for a company publication. He bestowed the award to a prominent American in a ceremony at the Waldorf Astoria. One year, he presented the award to J. Robert Oppenheimer, who headed the Manhattan Project that developed the atomic bomb.

Cheatham acquired a Rolls Royce, which his daughter recalls was a dashing automobile with some persistent mechanical problems. "He was so proud of it. It was a beautiful car. It had something like 38 coats of paint to get it the color blue he wanted, but I think that Rolls Royce spent more time in the shop than on the road."

The idea for the Rolls likely came from Ben Sonnenberg, a flashy New York publicist and party-giver who, according to *Maverick*, once told Cheatham, "Owen, you're not sitting in a front porch rocking chair in Georgia. You're in New York City now and you've got to act like you're in New York City." Sonnenberg helped Cheatham secure membership in a club called The Brook as well as The Links Club, reserved the couple a box at the Metropolitan Opera and introduced Celeste into the Mardi Gras Ball.

Cheatham's coup de grace in New York was purchasing the Dali Jewels, elaborate pieces of jewelry fashioned after the paintings of the surrealistic artist Salvador Dali. Cheatham bought them for The Owen Cheatham Foundation and sent them on tours around the world, showcasing them to raise money for charities. "There were only about 12 jewels at first, but we commissioned more from Charles Valiant & Co. — there were 37 in all," Celeste says.

The Cheathams exported their social charm to the West Coast when Georgia-Pacific moved to Portland, where they purchased a lavish estate named "Blueberry Hill," a 20-room Georgian-style mansion surrounded by what one reporter called "eight acres of putting-green lawn."

At Blueberry Hill, Cheatham would hold annual press conferences. After cocktails, Cheatham would hold court. "Flanked by lesser corporate lights, Cheatham would make a brief speech and then field questions in a charming though somewhat condescending style, according to some reporters who attended," wrote Anthony Bianco, a Portland reporter. "For Oregon, this was something new," Gerry Pratt wrote in the *Oregonian*. Also new to Oregon was the formality of Cheatham's office — with a shoeshine man making regular rounds.

The press conferences at Blueberry Hill were only a blip in the ongoing social whirl. "The parties at the Cheathams' were lavish," recalls Robert Flowerree, who joined Georgia-Pacific in 1952 and later became chairman and CEO. "They were always black-tie. Owen insisted on

Owen Cheatham entrance hall.

SUNDAY, APRIL 13, 1969

The Owen R. Cheatham Apartment
River House, New York City

Mrs. Cheatham's blue and yellow bedroom in New York. The chaise is cherry color velvet.

The Owen Cheatham library in soft greens and reds.

Photos—Jerome Zerbe

The Living Room.

New York was the primary residence for the Cheathams because Celeste Cheatham could not fly. In the city, the Cheathams traveled in a Rolls Royce and lived in a lavish apartment with their two daughters, Celeste, above, and Mary Fenton.

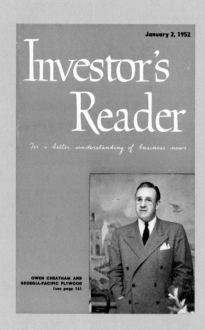

January 2, 1952

Investor's Reader

For a better understanding of business news

OWEN CHEATHAM AND
GEORGIA-PACIFIC PLYWOOD
(see page 16)

As Georgia-Pacific grew and its shares became a boom stock, Cheatham received increasing press attention, such as this cover of *Investor's Reader*. A San Francisco banker described Cheatham as "one of the greatest and brightest people living." In Portland, the Cheathams lived in a 20-room mansion called "Blueberry Hill" on eight acres of meticulously tended lawn, opposite. There they hosted elegant black-tie parties for several nights in a row.

that. He insisted on strict attire for people working for the company. Coat and tie at work. Black tie for parties. At Blueberry Hill, he would invite the officers to discuss business. The ladies would go into a different room. The men would have coffee. And then he gave big parties and dances with orchestras."

Alyce Cheatham recalls that the parties at Blueberry Hill would go on for days, with different parties held almost in shifts.

"They were fantastic, and they were probably Portland's most elegant parties," Alyce Cheatham recalls. "Owen would have three parties in a row, for their friends, for the officers and for the directors of Georgia-Pacific. No one understood how they could do it."

Making the scene in Portland was difficult for Owen's wife, who could not travel by airplane. Her daughter explained that Mrs. Cheatham's ears were damaged by a childhood case of scarlet fever and she couldn't bear the pressure of an elevator ride to the top of the Empire State Building, much less ride in an airplane. As a result, she took the train to Portland and all her overseas travel was by ocean liner.

The Cheatham's daughter Celeste often accompanied her father on trips because her mother could not fly. The daughters and their mother considered New York home and traveled to Portland only for special occasions.

"But Daddy adored Portland," Celeste recalls. "I used to say to him, 'Oh, it rains all the time out here.' He said, 'Well, that's good because it makes the trees grow.'"

Owen and Celeste Cheatham were not the typical Portland couple, Alyce Cheatham recalls. "They lived a more social lifestyle. They were very sophisticated and

very glamorous. Celeste was a fantastically intelligent and talented woman. She was a decorator in New York and had a beautiful collection of antiques. She was always helping her friends and family. She would call and say, 'I have these really special things here. I think they'd go nicely in your house.' She wasn't putting you on. She really was sincere. She helped a lot of us learn the essentials of decorating."

Cheatham's daughter recalls that no matter how sophisticated and worldly her father became, he retained the humble religion of the country boy he once was. "He was a very religious man," she says. "He would get down on his knees at night and pray. He'd always go to church. He was a very good man — a really good man."

In 1960, much of Cheatham's world came crashing down when he suffered a stroke while in Washington, D.C. "He was checking into a hotel in Washington, and he was by himself," Celeste says. "He later told me, 'I couldn't say anything. I went up to check in and the people at the desk didn't know what to do.' He knew what he wanted to say, but he couldn't say it. My mother and I went down on the train. By this time, they had him in the hospital."

Cheatham was partially paralyzed for a while but overcame the paralysis and eventually returned to work, although Celeste acknowledges that her father "was not quite as sharp" after the stroke. He retired at age 65, in 1967.

Cheatham suffered a heart attack after he retired but remained active. He returned to Portland for a board meeting in the fall of 1970 and went to Eugene, Oregon, to watch a University of Oregon football game with friends. "They were playing the 'The Star Spangled Banner' and

they were standing up, and all of a sudden, someone looked around and Daddy's eyes just went up into his head. He collapsed, and everybody rushed around. They got him to the hospital — but it just wasn't in time," Celeste says.

Cheatham's wife did not last long without her husband. "My mother just became very ill after my father died," says Celeste Cheatham. "To this day, we don't really know what my mother died of. Maybe she died of a broken heart. She loved being Mrs. Owen Cheatham."

In 2000, The Owen Cheatham Foundation and Georgia-Pacific agreed to work jointly on a project to honor Cheatham's memory at the Georgia Golf Hall of Fame in Augusta, Georgia. The memorial will include a plaque honoring Cheatham in a garden — surrounded by trees.

But G-P took a long-term approach to the timber-lands, instituting a policy of "dynamic conservation" — cutting old timber, but replanting new trees — and building additional facilities. By 1960, the year that Toledo was supposed to die, its employment was up 50 percent and its payrolls up 100 percent.

Cheatham strongly believed that the future of the industry was in second-growth timber. This flew in the face of the existing philosophy of lumbermen that once the old-growth timber was exhausted, the industry would simply die. He realized that the growth of Douglas fir began to slow after it was 80 to 90 years old. He saw from burned-over lands where trees had regenerated that second-growth timber that was 80 years old would yield more wood than 200-year-old trees.

He became convinced that the industry should cut the old growth and make way for young, healthy timber. Georgia-Pacific put the dynamic conservation philosophy into practice, even though its competitors did not. Cheatham also realized that millions of board feet of timber was being left in the woods as waste. He saw that timber unsuitable for plywood or lumber could be used as wood fiber for such products as particleboard and in the pulp and paper industry. He believed he could turn old Northwest timberlands into a much more profitable investment than they previously had been.

As G-P planned to expand its timber holdings, Pamplin devised an ingenious method of taking huge loans to buy large tracts of timber and then quickly cutting and selling off a portion of the timber to pay

off the loans. When the loans were paid, G-P owned the land and the remaining timber.

This approach caused some controversy because the rapid cutting of timber led in some cases to disruption in local tax bases designed for longer-term cutting policies, and, ultimately, to mill closings and job loss. But G-P also aggressively reforested the lands where it was cutting trees. Most acquisitions, like C. D. Johnson, typically boosted both employment and sales.

The first deal under Pamplin's acquisition plan came in 1954, when Georgia-Pacific paid $12 million to acquire 19,000 acres of timberlands and a sawmill near the Toledo operation. Most of the older timber was liquidated under cutting contracts to repay the loans.

Pamplin also devised another scheme as G-P stock became more valuable. If a seller wanted $30 million for a property that G-P thought was worth only $25 million, "We would say, 'We will give you $25 million and we will put in escrow $5 million of Georgia-Pacific stock. If it doesn't get to where you would get the extra $5 million in three years, then we will give you sufficient stock to bring it up to $30 million,'" Pamplin later explained. In those days, the stock always rose enough to fulfill the agreement.

Pamplin said he discontinued the practice when the federal government informed the company that it would have to account for the shares held in escrow as outstanding. The practice was discontinued in the late 1950s, at the end of G-P's major buying spree. As Pamplin put it, "The government said, 'If you put them in there, from here on, you've got to show them as outstanding.' Well, that occurred at about the tail end of what we had done. And in the future we didn't need that."

Also in 1954, the company got into fierce competition for the Oregon-Mesabi tracts, 23,000 acres of forest containing a billion board feet of timber and owned by the Boeing family of Seattle, who wanted $12.5 million cash. U.S. Plywood also wanted the property badly. Cheatham and Pamplin knew the timing of their bid was critical. They had just one weekend to put together the deal with their bankers.

"We phoned a banker or two on Friday after-noon," Cheatham wrote, "and the following Monday morning one of our representatives walked into Boeing's bank in Seattle to see the agent for the Boeing timber. As he entered the office, a group of Wall Street financiers were coming out but the man discovered the timber was still for sale. 'Well,' said the agent. 'I suppose you don't have the $12.5 million in cash either?' 'Wrong,' our man replied. 'It is already deposited right here in your own bank.' And it was."

The investment-banking firm Blyth & Company had agreed to make the purchase and hold the prop-erty for six months for repayment of the principal plus $500,000 interest.

G-P made this deal under the nose of Lawrence Ottinger, founder of U.S. Plywood, who was furious when the upstarts from G-P beat him to the prime timber. Five years later, the companies would butt heads again when the stakes were much higher.

Perhaps the greatest weapon was Cheatham's

connections a continent away with bankers and insurance companies who would lend him the money and with the brokers who sold his stock. "Georgia-Pacific developed the finest relationships with national financial institutions of any company in the Northwest because they worked hard on it," Bill Boone, a Portland stockbroker, told *Willamette Week*. "Owen Cheatham had an office on Riverside Drive in New York and he invited every broker in the business to come and see him."

The company arrived with its aggressively creative financing at a time when aging timber barons were looking to sell, often with Jimmy Miller of Blyth & Co. as the middleman.

Still, the little company from Georgia was viewed with utter disdain by the timber barons of the Northwest. Georgia-Pacific's new and successful strategy was brazen compared with the staid and unchanging industry it had invaded only a few years earlier, and its remarkable growth spawned intense jealously among the people G-P was passing by, who began accusing the company of being exploitative.

Talmadge recalls the resentment G-P encountered in Portland. "The lumber families got the idea that we were a 'cut and get out' company," Talmadge says. "And some of the big lumber families were not very nice, or just ignored you. One man who was big in Booth-Kelly said he would never sell his home to anybody from Georgia-Pacific. And he never did."

"Cut and get out" was an ugly epithet for a lumber company, raising visions of a rapacious sweep through virgin timberlands, leaving behind a bare

As Georgia-Pacific began buying vast tracts of timberland in the Pacific Northwest, Owen Cheatham adopted a philosophy he called "dynamic conservation." He realized that the future of the forest products industry was in second-growth timber. While G-P aggressively cut timber, it also aggressively replanted young trees. Cheatham also realized that millions of board feet of timber were being left in the woods as waste. He saw that timber unsuitable for plywood or lumber could be used as wood fiber for such products as particleboard and in the pulp and paper industry. Through dynamic conservation and creative use of "waste" wood, Cheatham was able to get more value from the land.

1956

America's wealth
lies in her
growing things

Whether it is people, companies or natural resources . . . growth underlies the strength of our nation. Therein, lies the Georgia-Pacific story—strength from its *living* resource—timber.

Through progressive forest management, timber's year-to-year growth becomes a *perpetual* resource. Through Georgia-Pacific research, timber's value increases with every new product discovery from wood and wood fiber: plywood, plastic, lumber, pulp, paper, chemicals... and more to come with Georgia-Pacific's increasing utilization of each log!

Georgia-Pacific anticipated America's hunger for growing things, and today is the careful custodian of one of the finest and largest timber reserves in private ownership . . . a living resource that assures constant growth and increasing value. *For descriptive booklet, write to Georgia-Pacific Corporation, 270 Park Avenue, New York 17, N.Y.*

Ten years of sales growth

MILLIONS OF DOLLARS

120 · 100 · 80 · 60 · 40 · 20 · 0

1946 1949 1952 1955

GEORGIA—PACIFIC
CORPORATION

GEORGIA-PACIFIC PLYWOOD COMPANY
GEORGIA-PACIFIC PAPER COMPANY

Quality forest products since 1927

swath of land. It was an unfair characterization of G-P by its competitors. "The reason people resented Georgia-Pacific," Flowerree explains, "was that G-P paid a lot more for timber than was currently being paid and the company was able to successfully merchandise it," he says. "People resented the success more than anything. They saw somebody come in from the outside and succeed — and they didn't like it."

Indeed, Georgia-Pacific swept into Washington and Oregon so swiftly and aggressively that it would stir up hard feelings that were barely ameliorated by the time the company moved back South a quarter-century later. "The rapid rise of G-P from its Oregon base is one of the great corporate success stories of the postwar era," wrote Anthony Bianco in a 1979 series for *Willamette Week*. "It is a story of unmatched financial ingenuity, high-level salesmanship, uncanny timing, far-sighted business acumen, cunning and sheer guts. But it is also — among other things — the story of a public-relations nightmare. G-P created thousands of jobs and pumped hundreds of millions of dollars into the Oregon economy in salaries and capital investment, but in so doing it managed to antagonize virtually the entire state."

PUTTING TALENT TO WORK

While critics continued to snub their noses at the upstarts from Georgia, the company was not only surviving the low prices of plywood, it was figuring out how to thrive. In 1954, the company earned $1.8 million on sales of $62 million. In 1955, its sales jumped almost a third, but earnings soared even more substantially — they tripled.

That year, Georgia-Pacific began supplementing shareholders' cash dividends with stock. "This policy permits the company to retain a large portion of its cash earnings for expansion and development and at the same time to provide its stockholders with substantial income," Cheatham wrote in the 1955 annual report. The 1955 payment of $1 per share in cash plus 6 percent in stock at the current market value represented a total dividend worth $4 per share, Cheatham said. The system was a boon to shareholders, providing a substantial increase over the 1954 annual dividend of 25 cents a share for common stock holders.

Cheatham and Pamplin began growing their team. Cheatham reinstated Pamplin to the board and Robert Flowerree was elevated to a vice presidential position. The next year, Pamplin was elected to the executive committee. The company also brought in Jack Brandis, a hulking former Oregon State College fullback, to be executive vice president in charge of timber, production and sales of West Coast operations. And they hired a gregarious accountant named Harry Kane from Arthur Andersen & Co.

The influx of new talent arrived just in time. In 1956, Georgia-Pacific would triple its timber holdings from four billion feet to more than twelve billion feet.

Brandis was instrumental in two major acquisitions, the $70 million purchase of the Coos Bay Lumber Company, which owned 120,000 acres of timberland with four billion feet of old-growth Douglas fir, and the $75 million acquisition of

Hammond Lumber Company, which owned 127,000 acres of redwood timber in Humboldt County, California, representing another four billion feet of timber. Much of the financing came from bank loans secured by cutting contracts.

With Coos Bay, Brandis overcame some of G-P's early concerns by convincing the officers that they could use all the timber, even the diseased Douglas fir known as "white speck." Most companies in the industry disdained white speck as worthless, but Brandis used it to make plywood. Competitors joked that "you could throw a cat through Jack Brandis' plywood," but Brandis believed there was a market for "economy" plywood. An industry trade group opposed it, but G-P, ever the maverick, plunged

In 1956, the company changed its name again to Georgia-Pacific Corporation, reflecting the addition of pulp and paper to its portfolio. A print ad from that year includes the new name as well as impressive growth figures. The company more than tripled its holdings with its acquisition of Coos Bay Lumber Company for $70 million and Hammond Lumber Company, above, for $75 million. Each of the new companies held four billion feet of timber.

forward and salvaged timber that other previous owners had scorned.

"Jack opened a whole market for it," recalls Robert Flowerree. "The distribution division was happy because they could sell it for less than regular plywood. They could move it quickly and sold a lot of it. Before Jack, it was just thrown away."

Flowerree characterized G-P's desire to use every bit of timber as "getting more squeal from the hog." Cheatham called it getting "everything but the rustle" from the tree. Whatever they called it, the Coos Bay and Hammond acquisitions doubled the company's plywood production and exposed the need for a top-flight sales manager. As usual, the company turned to talent maven Julian Cheatham, who recruited William H. Hunt from U.S. Plywood.

When Hunt walked into his new office in Portland, he found it ready for him, complete with pencils, paper and a request from Pamplin for recommendations on

a new distribution system within 36 hours. Hunt met this request with a plan to change the warehouses from terminals to wholesale centers for the distribution of building materials, each an independent profit center. He created a policy for the distribution division to sell 120 percent of G-P production so they would keep G-P mills running when markets were weak, similar to Owen Cheatham's selling style during the Depression.

Georgia-Pacific spent $145 million in just three months on Coos Bay and Hammond. The company's debt had soared to three times G-P's net worth in 1956. But in the five years after the purchase of C. D. Johnson, the value of standing timber had doubled, and would double again before the end of the decade. The value of timber had been depressed from the 1920s until World War II, but the housing boom of the 1950s increased demand and drove up prices with surprising speed. Georgia-Pacific had gone on a timber-buying spree at precisely the right time.

"What is perhaps most remarkable about G-P's success is not that it was able to assemble a vast reserve of prime old-growth timber with such rapidity, but rather that it had virtually no competition," Anthony Bianco wrote in *Willamette Week*. He noted that Weyerhaeuser already presided over the largest private timber reserve in America and believed it didn't need any more. By the end of the 1950s, however, Weyerhaeuser was free of long-term debt, while G-P wallowed in it.

In 1957, Robert Pamplin was elected president of the company. Robert Flowerree began making his

IA – PACIFIC

inished
neling

TINCTIVE, NEW
OD WALL PANELS

GEORGIA – PACIFIC
PLYWOOD COMPANY

As the plywood market boomed, Georgia-Pacific hired Robert O. Lee in 1956 as director of advertising. He developed literature, such as the photo at left, to promote the company's products. Plywood enjoyed an enormous range of uses, from interior paneling, right, to providing forms for pouring concrete at huge construction projects, below.

Georgia-Pacific continued its relentless growth in 1959. The company entered a bitterly fought competition with U.S. Plywood to buy Booth-Kelly Lumber Company of Springfield, Oregon, which had 3.3 billion board feet of prime Douglas fir. In the biggest drama of Owen Cheatham's career, G-P prevailed, ultimately paying $93 million for Booth-Kelly.

mark as well, leading G-P into pulp and paper with the construction of a $22 million mill at Toledo, fed by waste chips. It was the only pulp and paper mill G-P ever built — all the others were acquired. The move into pulp and paper was an integral part of G-P's integration strategy, finding a way to use every bit of the tree. Chips that formerly were burned as waste in old-fashioned wigwam burners could now be mixed with water and fashioned into a full range of paper products.

"One day, Owen came in and said, 'We're going to get into the paper business. I want you to build a mill in Toledo,'" Flowerree recalls. "A real concern for all of us was what to do with the paper after we'd made it. Owen hired Stewart Daniels, a vice president of Union Bag at the time. He did a real good job of finding markets for us."

Flowerree wasn't surprised that he was virtually left alone to manage the construction of a $20 million mill. The remarkable autonomy was simply the way things were done at G-P. "It all worked out pretty well," he says. "Owen was busy with the big picture. As long as the figures were okay, he left you alone. In those days, everybody in G-P was his own man."

In 1959, Georgia-Pacific resumed its relentless growth with an attempt to acquire Booth-Kelly Lumber Company, which *Willamette Week* described as "G-P's Oregon coup de grace."

Booth-Kelly owned 18 percent of Springfield Plywood Company, one of G-P's earliest West Coast investments. Booth-Kelly was to supply logs for Springfield and, in return, take a percentage of plywood. But neither party was happy with the agreement. When Booth-

Booth Kelly Lumber Co.
SPRINGFIELD, OREGON

Kelly's president, Eliot Jenkins, offered to buy Springfield, Cheatham grew suspicious that Booth-Kelly had not made good on its end of the deal. Cheatham suspected Jenkins had withheld peeler logs from the plant in order to dry up the supply of local logs, intending to make the Springfield operation less viable and Georgia-Pacific more willing to part with its interest in the joint venture. In 1956, G-P sued Booth-Kelly to enforce the contract, and Booth-Kelly filed suit arguing the mill was not operated in its interest.

Jimmy Miller of Blyth & Co. alerted Cheatham in 1959 when he heard that Booth-Kelly was for sale, with its 3.3 billion board feet of prime Douglas fir on land that had already been developed for logging.

Cheatham flew to Chicago to make an offer, but the Booth-Kelly board of directors rejected it. Jenkins announced that the Booth-Kelly board was planning to sell the company to U.S. Plywood. Cheatham quickly upped the ante, but the Booth-Kelly directors announced they had agreed to sell the company's properties to U.S. Plywood for $85.5 million.

Cheatham and Pamplin decided to fight back.

G-P sprang into action in the courts. Amid a flurry of lawsuits and negotiations, the company acquired a list of Booth-Kelly stockholders. "We decided to appeal directly to the Booth-Kelly stockholders, offering to buy their stock at a per-share price, which would top our competitor's bid," Cheatham wrote. G-P officers contacted the 144 Booth-Kelly stockholders, ran newspaper advertisements in several cities and upped the offer to $93 million. U.S. Plywood would not budge

beyond its original offer, so G-P obtained 98 percent of Booth-Kelly stock.

The Booth-Kelly deal showcased what *Fortune* magazine described in May 1962 as Georgia-Pacific's "peculiarly aggressive style." According to *Fortune*, G-P tied up the Booth-Kelly stock while Owen Cheatham was involved in lengthy discussions with U.S. Plywood, whose representatives "were enraged, and accused G-P's representatives of negotiating in bad faith." Cheatham offered U.S. Plywood one-third of Booth-Kelly, at whatever price G-P had paid, but U.S. Plywood representatives refused to take part in any further dealing, *Fortune* said.

G-P already had placed the $93 million in escrow in banks around the country. According to *Fortune*, G-P's mode of financing the Booth-Kelly deal "was almost as intriguing to timbermen as the property itself." The $93 million was borrowed for a mere six months from several banks, according to *Fortune*, and was repaid in three ways: "First, the Georgia-Pacific Timber Co., a G-P subsidiary, obtained $45 million from selling off portions of the Booth-Kelly timber outright. Second, it obtained $39 million of long-term credit from the Chase Manhattan Bank, First National City Bank and the Bank of America, secured by a timber-harvesting agreement…. Third, there was $9 million of Booth-Kelly's own cash and securities. After it had control, G-P had to dig up still another $5 million for the operating needs of the new subsidiary."

In 1960, with its debt at an enormous level following the Booth-Kelly acquisition, G-P tried yet another

In a 1960 *Forbes* magazine cover story, a Wall Street source declared, "Owen Cheatham is one of the few authentic geniuses in American industry today." Cheatham also was close to several U.S. Presidents, including Lyndon B. Johnson and Richard M. Nixon.

THE WHITE HOUSE

WASHINGTON

March 13, 1967

Dear Mr. Cheatham:

Thank you for your endorsement of our move to restore the investment credit.

I recall your concern on this subject and want you to know that I will continue to watch all the developments closely. My efforts will be easier because of the knowledge of your thoughtful and cooperative partnership.

Sincerely,

Mr. Owen R. Cheatham
Chairman of the Board
Georgia-Pacific Corporation
375 Park Avenue
New York, New York 10022

FORBES MAGAZINE

OFFICE OF THE PRESIDENT

January 16, 1968

Mr. Owen R. Cheatham
Chairman of the Board
Georgia-Pacific Corporation
375 Park Avenue
New York, New York 10022

Dear Owen:

I have just read No.3, Volume 8 on "Growth."

What a terrific story. . . and all accomplished at a time when so many were proclaiming that it was no longer possible to achieve what you subsequently have achieved, and, on such a fabulous scale!

With warmest affection,

As ever,

Malcolm S. Forbes

MSF:es

FORBES BUILDING   60 FIFTH AVENUE   NEW YORK, N.Y. 10011

creative method of financing to acquire a 13,000-acre tract of timberland in Southern Oregon owned by the Timber Conservation Company. Instead of borrowing more money, G-P acquired the land for $8.4 million through a member of its board of directors, Carrol Shanks, president of Prudential Insurance Company, a former Yale law professor and co-author of four books with Supreme Court Justice William O. Douglas.

Shanks borrowed $3.9 million from Bank of America and G-P threw in $4.4 million in cash, according to *Willamette Week*. Having bought the company, Shanks sold it immediately to a subsidiary of G-P for the sale price plus interest. Dick West, a G-P board member who represented the law firm Shearman & Sterling, warned that the deal could appear to be a conflict of interest. And, in fact, a *Wall Street Journal* reporter later won a Pulitzer Prize for writing about the arrangement. Although the New Jersey Banking and Insurance Commission cleared the transaction, the appearance of wrongdoing drove Shanks to retire from Prudential.

Also in 1960, Georgia-Pacific acquired W. M. Ritter Lumber Company, the Virginia company that had originally refused to hire the young Owen Cheatham nearly 40 years earlier. It was the most important Southern acquisition by G-P up to that time. Cheatham said the principal target was Appalachian hardwoods, with the additional value of substantial deposits of natural gas and coal beneath the timberlands. The company leased the mineral rights on a royalty basis.

In the same year, as the new decade of the 1960s dawned, one of Georgia-Pacific's guiding lights was suddenly dimmed. Cheatham suffered an aneurysm in a carotid artery and underwent emergency surgery in Washington, D.C. He never fully recovered, although the company never revealed his condition to the press or stockholders.

"It slowed him down tremendously," recalls Marion Talmadge. "After that, he'd look at you and maybe call you by another name that wasn't yours."

Sidelined for nearly a year by his condition, Cheatham kept his titles of chairman and chief executive officer, and remained headquartered in New York. He recovered well enough to continue his relationships with bankers and to resume his active social life in New York, Portland and Palm Beach.

But from that point on, Robert Pamplin ran Georgia-Pacific from the Portland headquarters.

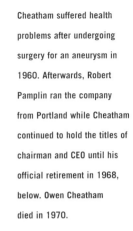

Cheatham suffered health problems after undergoing surgery for an aneurysm in 1960. Afterwards, Robert Pamplin ran the company from Portland while Cheatham continued to hold the titles of chairman and CEO until his official retirement in 1968, below. Owen Cheatham died in 1970.

No one complained because the company's growth remained phenomenal. With the acquisition of W. M. Ritter Lumber Co. in 1960, Georgia-Pacific had accumulated one million acres of timberland. Between 1954 and 1960, G-P had spent nearly $300 million on timberlands and $60 million on expansion and modernization of plants to use the timber for lumber, plywood, hardboard, wood chips, pulp and paper.

By 1962, sales had increased five times to $324 million from $63 million a decade earlier. Profits had increased 10 times to $19 million from $1.9 million in 1952.

Pamplin remained an outdoorsman, harking back to his early years on the farm in Virginia. In Portland, he often turned over his weekend kill to company cooks to prepare for the officers for lunch. Even as he became a multi-millionaire, some of his tastes remained primitive.

Treasurer Marion Talmadge recalls going hunting and fishing in Georgia with Pamplin, who prepared their meals.

"One of the things we shot was squirrels," Talmadge says. "Bob made a dish with the squirrel. He skinned the thing and dressed it out, then boiled it in water and put other things in with it, like Saltine crackers, and it got to be a thick soup. I looked down and there were these eyes floating around on top of it. I couldn't eat a thing."

Flowerree, on the other hand, was much more refined in tastes and manner. Invariably described as a

With the acquisition of W. M. Ritter Lumber Co. in 1960, Georgia-Pacific had accumulated one million acres of timberland. Between 1954 and 1960, G-P had spent nearly $300 million on timberlands and $60 million on expansion and modernization of plants to use the timber for lumber, plywood, hardboard, wood chips, pulp and paper.

Georgia-Pacific increasingly integrated its operations, using more and more of the tree to produce plywood, paper, textiles, chemicals and other products in addition to lumber. Wood fiber chips — called "Green Gold," at G-P — were converted to paper at the Bellingham, Washington, operation, left. While expanding and integrating, the company continued to be a leading producer of lumber, its original product, and veneers, seen above in the manufacturing process.

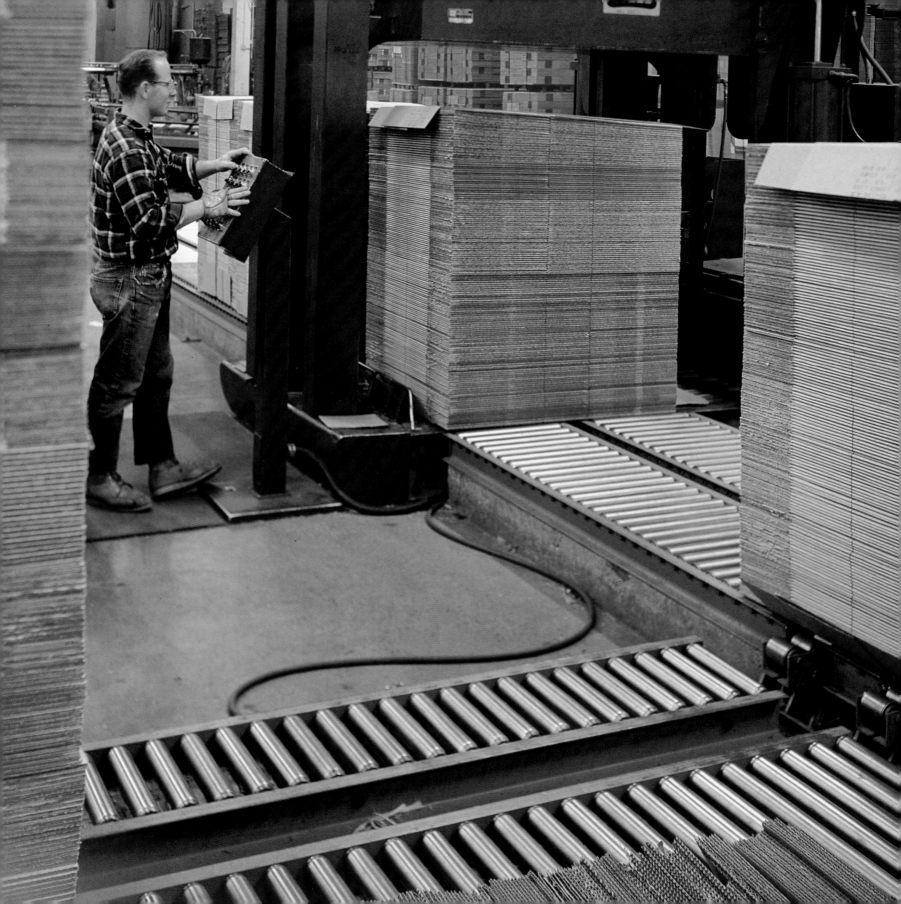

genuine Southern gentleman, Flowerree's accent flowed with a soft touch of the bayous. He earned a psychology degree from Tulane University in New Orleans and served as a Navy lieutenant in the Pacific during World War II. The scion of a wealthy family, he was dispatched to the Northwest in 1947 to represent his grandfather's interests in C. D. Johnson Lumber Company and to learn the lumber business.

Flowerree and Pamplin had once roomed together when the company first moved its headquarters from Olympia to Portland. "We were very close. Bob and I worked together and had the same philosophies," Flowerree said. It was his task to expand the company's business through the process of integration.

INTEGRATING

Integrating operations meant Georgia-Pacific owned the timberlands, harvested the timber, converted it to finished products and produced some of the wood-based chemicals used in manufacturing and then sold what it made.

Flowerree's first step was to get into the pulp and paper business at Toledo, which at the time was not only a venture into a new line of business but also a touch of revenge. G-P had been selling chips from the Toledo operation to Longview Fiber Company, which was paying 25 cents a unit and wouldn't budge from that price.

"We thought we weren't getting enough," Flowerree said in a taped TV interview for the company. "Jim Buckley and I went up to Longview Fiber

Company one time and tried to get them to raise the price; they just laughed at us. I think that's what really was a deciding factor. We were so irked at Longview Fiber Company, we said 'The heck with it. We'll build our own mill.'"

That 250-ton-a-day mill was profitable almost from the day it began operating, in 1957, converting what once was either burned as waste or sold to Longview into $5 million in profits as paper.

In 1961, Flowerree then built a corrugated container plant in Olympia, Washington, where Olympia Brewing agreed to hire G-P to produce part of its packaging. He acquired National Box and Specialty Company of Sheboygan, Wisconsin, and Oshkosh Corrugated Box Manufacturing Company of Oshkosh, Wisconsin.

With the help of Albert G. Naudain, who Stuart Daniels had recruited from Union Bag, Flowerree worked out a contract with William Mitchell, president of the Safeway grocery chain. G-P would build and operate a kraft paper bag and sacks plant. Safeway would lease the plant and buy the bags and sacks. The agreement circumvented an agreement G-P had with the Cupples Company not to sell grocery bags on the West Coast.

At Coos Bay, Oregon, Flowerree entered the resin business in 1959 through an agreement with Reichhold Chemical Company, which enabled Georgia-Pacific to make its own resins. The process saved the company $1,500 the first week and provided resins for the plywood plants as well. Georgia-Pacific was now in the chemicals business.

Another Georgia-Pacific product introduced in the 1960s was corrugated containers. An employee moves along stacks of containerboard at a G-P plant, opposite. The containerboard is converted into corrugated boxes, seen coming off a production line, above. The boxes have a myriad of uses in packaging consumer items throughout the economy, from simple shipping boxes for paper products and manufactured goods to specialty waxed boxes for the sanitary shipment of poultry and produce.

In 1962, Georgia-Pacific paid $125 million to acquire the mammoth Crossett Lumber Company in Crossett, Arkansas, a quintessential mill town that grew up around the company formed in 1899. In true G-P tradition, it didn't take the company long to "paint it blue." An Oregon state flag is hoisted over what was once a Crossett Lumber building, above, as the G-P logo already adorns the front of the building.

THE CROSSETT ACQUISITION

Flowerree made the decision to get Georgia-Pacific into the tissue business as a result of the company's largest and most significant acquisition in the South, Crossett Lumber Company, based in an old-fashioned mill town, Crossett, Arkansas. Crossett owned more than 500,000 acres of timberland in the remote southeast corner of Arkansas.

Crossett Lumber Company had been created in 1899 and ran a classic, benevolent company town until World War II, owning all stores, the homes of workers and even the schools, which the company operated. After the war, the company sold the housing to the workers. Crossett Lumber also "pioneered in forest conservation practices far in advance of its time, and became a showcase for such practices," according to a 1981 Masters thesis by George Walter Balogh at the University of Arkansas titled "Crossett, Arkansas: The History of A Forest Industry, A Community and Change."

In 1926, the year before Owen Cheatham formed Georgia Hardwood, Crossett hired W. K. Williams, a forestry graduate of Yale University, who immediately initiated a program of sustained yield for the company. With considerable assistance from Yale, Williams began a program to perpetuate Crossett's forest by harvesting trees at a rate no greater than the growth rate of the trees. It was one of the most progressive policies in the nation at that time.

By 1960, Crossett Lumber was owned by heirs of the three founders: E. S. Crossett, J. W. Watzek and C. W. Gates. The Crossett family, which owned

26 percent of the stock, decided to sell.

Peter Watzek, president of Crossett, agreed to sell the property to Union Bag for a total of $156 million or $68.50 per share. (Union Bag later became the Union Camp Corporation, which was acquired by International Paper in 1999.) But Alexander Calder Jr., president of Union Camp, became concerned about the price as well as a threatened investigation by the Federal Trade Commission for a possible antitrust violation if the deal went through. He terminated the negotiations.

The ubiquitous Jimmy Miller of Blyth & Co. represented the Crossett family and was instructed to offer the company to Weyerhaeuser, but its officers felt the price was outrageously high. Under pressure to sell the Crossett family's stock, Miller contacted Pamplin, who flew to New York and agreed to buy the Crossett shares for $47.50 per share — more than $20 less than the early Union Bag offer — and said he would pay $55 per share if he were able to buy over 50 percent of the outstanding shares.

The Watzeks were reluctant to sell to G-P, fearing the worst for the company and the town that was so tightly linked with it. According to Balogh's thesis, a branch of the Watzek family in Oregon "had viewed Georgia-Pacific's activities in the Booth-Kelly acquisition with suspicion."

Once G-P owned the Crossett family shares, however, the Watzeks sold their shares as well. By July 1962, G-P accumulated 99 percent of the stock at $55 per share. Harry Kane raised the $125 million through an interim financing arrangement.

The chemical complex at Crossett, Arkansas, left, helped Georgia-Pacific eventually become the forest products industry's leading supplier of wood resins, pine chamicals and specialty chemicals. The chemical facility can be seen on the following pages, in the lower right corner of the aerial picture of the vast Crossett Lumber complex, which included 565,000 acres of prime Southern timberlands. The Crossett forest, managed with the assistance of Yale University foresters, was considered far ahead of its time and was used as a showcase for conservation practices.

Welcome To Crossett GP Directors

The News Observer

Devoted to the best interests of Crossett and Ashley County

NOW TWICE WEEKLY

PUBLISHED IN CROSSETT, ARKANSAS—FORESTRY CAPITAL OF THE WORLD

MONDAY, APRIL 20, 1970   8 PAGES   10 CENTS

VOL. XXX   NO. 32

Robert B. Pamplin
Chairman & President
GP Corp.

Julian N. Cheatham
Exec. Vice-President
GP Corp.

Grayson M-P Murphy
Partner,
Shearman & Sterling

James F. Miller
President,
Blyth & Co., Inc.

James M. Halt
Chr. of the Board
FMC Corporation

Harvey C. Fruehauf, Jr.
Director and Pres.
The Fruehauf Foundation

Stuart T. Saunders
Chr. of the Board
Penn Central Company

John F. Watlington, Jr.
Pres. Wachovia Bank &
Trust Company N. A.

William H. Hunt
Exec. Vice-Pres.
GP Corp.

Harry J. Kane
Exec. Vice-Pres.,
GP Corp

Owen R. Cheatham
Honorary Chr. of the
Board and Chr. of the
Exec. Com., GP Corp.

S. Clark Beise
Former Director and Chr.
of the Exec. Com., Bank
of America N.T.&S.A.

Robert E. Floweree
Exec. Vice-Pres.
GP Corp.

The corporate officers of Georgia-Pacific Corporation have selected Crossett as the site for the company's April Board of Directors meeting and Annual Stockholders meeting to be held this week, April 21, 22, and 23. This is the first time since 1963 that the directors have visited Crossett, and only the second time for an annual Georgia-Pacific stockholders meeting in our city.

Crossett residents initially feared the Georgia-Pacific takeover because of the company's rugged reputation in the Northwest and its tough-ness during the Booth-Kelly acquisition. But the insular town eventually welcomed the new directors, above. According to one scholar, G-P handled the transition "tactfully and with a minimum of fuss." And G-P was now earning enough money that it did not have to finance growth through timber-cutting contracts.

Peter Watzek, the only descendent of the founding families who still lived in the company town, and his wife, Betty, left Crossett within a few days of the sale and only rarely returned, Balogh wrote. The rest of the Crossett Lumber management team stayed on when G-P took over.

Pamplin, as his acquisition strategy dictated, initially sold the rights to cut some of the Crossett timber, but he later bought back the rights. He no longer needed to liquidate timber. The purchase of Crossett Lumber was the beginning of a new era for Georgia-Pacific. The company was now earning enough money that it did not have to finance growth through timber-cutting contracts. After G-P paid $125 million for the complex, Kane refinanced the corporation's debt on a long-term basis. Cash flow now more than covered the annual debt obligations, so Kane could obtain financing on an unsecured basis.

But Georgia-Pacific's acquisition of Crossett sent chills through the tiny, close-knit community.

Davis Mortensen was a young engineer from Mississippi who had joined Crossett Lumber a year and a half before G-P bought it. "There were rumors all over town that Union Camp was trying to acquire Crossett," he recalls. "It was a small town. Everybody knew everybody. That fell through, and then there were rumors about Georgia-Pacific before they actually made the acquisition. I remember that the chairman and a lot of the top officers of the company came into Crossett to a dinner at the Rose Inn one evening and kind of laid out what they were going to do with Crossett to the local leaders.

"What I remember is that people in the town thought, 'Well, Georgia-Pacific is going to come in and cut all the trees out, and in about 10 years there won't be anything left of Crossett,'" Mortensen says. "They did not have a real good reputation. That was the way they were thought of at that time."

In an interview nearly 40 years after the acquisition, Mortensen chuckled as he recalled the fears. He had only recently retired from a long, distinguished career with Georgia-Pacific.

"Today, Crossett is much bigger than it was when Georgia-Pacific acquired it, and it still has as many trees," he says. "I can remember my boss at the time, Hiram Mersereau, telling me, 'This is going to be a

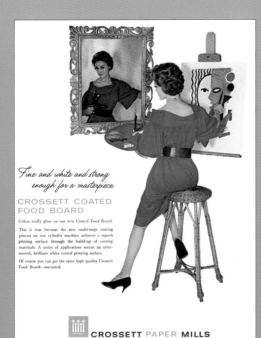

Fine and white and strong enough for a masterpiece.

CROSSETT COATED FOOD BOARD

Colors really glow on our new Coated Food Board.

This is true because the new multi-stage coating process on our cylinder machine achieves a superb printing surface through the build-up of coating materials. A series of applications means an ultra-smooth, brilliant white coated printing surface.

Of course you can get the same high quality Crossett Food Board—uncoated.

ᵐᵐ CROSSETT PAPER **MILLS**
A DIVISION OF THE CROSSETT COMPANY, CROSSETT, ARKANSAS, MAKERS OF PAPER, LUMBER, CHARCOAL AND CHEMICALS—ALL FROM MANAGED FORESTS.

For color packaging that looks good enough to eat...
CROSSETT COATED FOOD BOARD

Gown by Oleg Cassini

Your product's picture will have true appetite appeal when printed on new Crossett Coated Food Board. Multi-stage coating on our cylinder machine is the reason. Superb printing surface is achieved by the building up of coating materials in a series of applications that results in uniform coverage.

Smooth, strong and dazzling white, Crossett Coated Food Board will help you get fine printing, free of mottle, even on your most intricate jobs.

And of course you can get the same high quality Crossett Food Board—uncoated.

ᵐᵐ CROSSETT PAPER **MILLS**
A DIVISION OF THE CROSSETT COMPANY, CROSSETT, ARKANSAS, MAKERS OF PAPER, LUMBER, CHARCOAL AND CHEMICALS—ALL FROM MANAGED FORESTS.

Quality-controlled for your finest wrapping use...
CROSSETT LEATHERNECK WRAPPING PAPER

You can be sure of consistent quality in every weight of Crossett Leatherneck Wrapping Paper. You can be sure, too, of real savings. Our Basis Weight Control Program assures you maximum yards per ton at the strength you desire.

You will be pleased with the convenience of the new Cross-ett-Zip covering which features a built-in tear strip. No more cutting, no more wasted top layers of paper. One easy motion peels off the wrapper . . . lets clean, usable paper unwind from the first inch of the roll.

ᵐᵐ CROSSETT PAPER **MILLS**
A DIVISION OF THE CROSSETT COMPANY, CROSSETT, ARKANSAS, MAKERS OF PAPER, LUMBER, CHARCOAL AND CHEMICALS—ALL FROM MANAGED FORESTS.

Gown by Oleg Cassini

Custom-produced to meet your most imaginative needs

CROSSETT LEATHERNECK CONVERTING KRAFT

Order the weight and grade you want and Crossett will produce to your specifications. Our technical service will help you decide. There are real savings for you with our Basis Weight Control Program assuring maximum yards per ton at the strength you desire.

Crossett's Machine Time Plan lets regular customers "own the mill" for specified periods every month. Machine time can be reserved so you can obtain your Leatherneck Converting Kraft when you want it . . . at a fair price, whatever the state of the market.

ᵐᵐ CROSSETT PAPER **MILLS**
A DIVISION OF THE CROSSETT COMPANY, CROSSETT, ARKANSAS, MAKERS OF PAPER, LUMBER, CHARCOAL AND CHEMICALS – ALL FROM MANAGED FORESTS.

Slacks by Oleg Cassini

Advertisements for the Crossett Paper Mills indicated the breadth of the company's products, including kraft paper and wrapping paper. The entire Crossett complex made full use of its enormous forest, producing paper, plywood, lumber and chemicals. It even operated a short-line railroad to take its products to market.

Quality-controlled for your finest wrapping use...
CROSSETT LEATHERNECK WRAPPING PAPER

When you buy from Crossett you buy more wraps per ton at the strength you desire. The reason is our Basis Weight Control Program. For greater convenience the new Cross-ett-Zip covering features a built-in tear strip. No more cutting of the wrapper, no more wasted top layers of paper. One easy motion peels off the outer wrapper . . . lets clean, usable paper unwind from the first inch of the roll.

ᵐᵐ CROSSETT PAPER **MILLS**
A DIVISION OF THE CROSSETT COMPANY, CROSSETT, ARKANSAS, MAKERS OF PAPER, LUMBER, CHARCOAL AND CHEMICALS —ALL FROM MANAGED FORESTS.

Dress by Oleg Cassini

After seeing huge hardwood stands in the Crossett forest, Robert Flowerree decided to take Georgia-Pacific into the tissue business. To get the necessary tissue expertise, G-P acquired Vanity Fair Paper Mills in Plattsburgh, New York, in 1963. But the Weymss family refused to give up the Vanity Fair label, which G-P eventually acquired 37 years later when it acquired Fort James. Unable to use the name "Vanity Fair" in the 1960s, G-P coined the name "Coronet" for its new line of paper products. The company hired popular singer Rosemary Clooney, opposite, who promoted the product with the famous commercial jingle: "Extra value is what you get when you buy Coronet."

terrific opportunity for you, because of your age and what Georgia-Pacific is.' And it turned out to be a great opportunity for *him*, too. They acquired us in the summer of 1962, and in February of the following year, he was made vice president and moved to Augusta, Georgia, to head the Southern division. So it was a great opportunity for him and a lot of other people."

In his thesis, Balogh credited Georgia-Pacific with a smooth transition, saying G-P "managed to carry on the spirit of the old company despite its giant size and despite pressing concerns elsewhere. The transition from old to new was handled tactfully and with a minimum of fuss. The fears of the employees and citizens of the town were allayed by actions, not words."

LEARNING THE TISSUE BUSINESS

It was the vast timberlands at Crossett that led Georgia-Pacific into the tissue business, Flowerree recalls. "I got the idea about doing that. I saw all the oak they had. At that time, making tissue was about 80 percent hardwood and 20 percent softwood. And we had a problem of what to do with the oak. They had barely touched the volume of oak. I decided to get into the tissue business to use up a lot of the hardwoods there in Crossett."

But a minor problem arose. "We didn't know anything about the tissue business," Flowerree says. "So we bought Bobby Schumacher's company in New York and used their expertise."

"Bobby Schumacher's company" was Vanity Fair

Paper Mills in Plattsburgh, New York. Robert Schumacher was manager of the Plattsburgh plant and convinced the owners, his brothers-in-law, Charles and James Weymss, to sell the operation to G-P in 1963. The family refused to give up the Vanity Fair name, which was an established brand in the Northeast. Schumacher stayed with Georgia-Pacific and later rose to the positions of president and chief operating officer. Within a month of the merger, he came up with a new brand name for the tissue it was producing: "Coronet." Later, G-P chose the name "Delta" for tissue products sold in the South.

Also in 1963, Harry Kane and Owen Cheatham wooed Lawson Turcotte, president of Puget Sound Pulp and Timber Company, of Bellingham, Washington. Puget Sound Pulp and Timber owned the MD tissue brand, which had been established for nearly 40 years on the West Coast and also made tissue under private labels for Lucky Stores, Albertsons and Safeway.

Turcotte, a French Canadian and former soccer player, wanted $150 million. Turcotte and Kane later became fast friends, according to *Maverick*, "despite Kane's faux pas in arriving at the wrong Plaza Hotel to pick up Turcotte. When Kane found the right hotel, Turcotte asked the young man if he couldn't get his damn directions straight. Kane smilingly said he was trying."

Negotiations in New York failed, so Cheatham invited Turcotte to play golf at his estate in Palm Beach, Florida, where he finally agreed to an offer of $95 million in Georgia-Pacific common stock.

Turcotte accepted the deal despite opposition from his board, which may have stemmed from fear that G-P would close some operations, as it had closed some plywood operations in Bellingham in favor of other plywood plants elsewhere in the Georgia-Pacific system. But Turcotte made the deal because he saw that G-P now had adequate timber and wood fiber to operate Puget Sound Pulp and Timber.

With the addition of Puget Sound Pulp and Timber, G-P now had become a player in the tissue market. But some of the tissue salesmen did not stay with G-P, forcing the company to create a national marketing program. The national campaign drew criticism from Scott Paper Company, which announced concern about Georgia-Pacific's private-label, low-price business. Pamplin responded that G-P was not looking for a price war, but was confident that the company could survive one.

"We'll fight with anyone on any product under any conditions at any time," Pamplin warned. "And I think we'll do better."

But Flowerree and Schumacher, who became vice president of the new paper division, devised an alternative plan. G-P went after segments of the market where competition was weakest, such as bath tissue. Eugene Reed, who joined Georgia-Pacific in the Vanity Fair acquisition, developed the new brands for G-P while continuing the private-label business. To help market G-P's labels as they increased in popularity, Reed began using brokers, thus avoiding expensive advertising campaigns.

Also in 1963, Flowerree decided to build a

THE REDWOOD FOREST BATTLE

In the mid-1960s, the Sierra Club began a campaign to establish a national park for redwoods in northern California. The organization had targeted approximately 90,000 acres in an area where Georgia-Pacific held 30,000 acres of redwood timber.

Senate hearings began in June 1966 and three lumber companies — Miller Rellim, Arcata and Georgia-Pacific — continued their logging operations in the area until September, when they agreed to a one-year moratorium at the suggestion of G-P.

In June 1967, when the moratorium expired, Robert Pamplin told Senator Henry Jackson of Washington, a member of the Senate Interior Committee, that G-P would resume operations in the area. In October, G-P began hauling right-of-way trees cut in operations prior to 1965. Then G-P resumed cutting, although Pamplin agreed not to log within the proposed park area. In November, G-P began building a road into the McArthur-Elam Creek area, which the Sierra Club wanted included in the national park. The Sierra Club dubbed the area "the Emerald Mile."

Although G-P had been unable to obtain specific maps of the proposed park, it was careful to keep its cutting operations from 800 to 1,200 feet away from the area of dispute. Still, the Sierra Club denounced the action. Georgia-Pacific responded with a full-page ad in several national newspapers to show that redwoods already had been saved in several city, county and state parks. But the Sierra Club had already won the public relations war by establishing the idea that the national park was the last chance to save the redwoods and "the Emerald Mile."

In June 1969, Congress passed the bill to create a national redwood park. Georgia-Pacific reluctantly gave up 3,450 acres of timberland.

Although it came out on the short end of the publicity battle over the national park issue, Georgia-Pacific made a remarkable donation in 1969 to a more moderate conservation group. Georgia-Pacific donated 390 acres of redwoods on the Van Duzen River in northern California, valued at $6 million, to The Nature Conservancy. The land contained as many prime virgin redwoods as the land acquired for the Redwood National Park. Some of the trees were between 400 to 800 years old and were more than 15 feet in diameter.

Two of the groves were named for Owen R. Cheatham and Robert B. Pamplin.

It was the largest such gift in the history of the American conservation movement and, according to *Maverick*, it "brought from the editorial pages of the *Oregonian* an apology from the Northwest region for thinking so poorly of G-P when they first came to Oregon. G-P was not a 'cut and get out' operation after all."

Georgia-Pacific helped overcome its reputation as a "cut and run" operation with its donation of 390 acres of redwoods in Northern California to The Nature Conservancy in 1969. On the opposite page, Julian Cheatham (second from left), vice president of redwood operations at the time, watches the ceremonial planting of a seedling. The majestic second-growth redwoods at Fort Bragg, California, above, speak for themselves.

As the company continued growing in the 1960s, it acquired the beautiful holdings of St. Croix Paper Company in Woodland, Maine, which had nearly 620,000 acres of spruce and hardwood timber, above and right. The same year, 1963, G-P acquired Fordyce Lumber Company in Fordyce, Arkansas, which would play a crucial role in the expansion into Southern pine plywood.

500-ton-per-day pulp plant at Samoa, California, to use chips from redwood and Douglas fir, with the pulp to be sold on the world market.

Georgia-Pacific topped off a busy year by acquiring St. Croix Paper Company in Woodland, Maine, which had 619,999 acres of spruce and hardwood timber, and Fordyce Lumber Company, in Fordyce, Arkansas. The Fordyce facility would turn out to be a critical part of Georgia-Pacific's next big move.

ALCHEMY — SOUTHERN PINE PLYWOOD

With Georgia-Pacific controlling vast tracts of Southern timber in 1963, Robert Pamplin decided to run some experiments to determine the feasibility of using Southern pine to make sheathing plywood.

A long-accepted belief in the building products industry was that Douglas fir was the only tree suitable for making plywood. Other companies had made plywood from Southern pine before, but it was inferior to plywood made from fir. Experiments begun in 1952 at the Yale School of Forestry and the Forest Products Laboratory at Madison, Wisconsin, concluded that there was no feasible process for turning Southern pine into a comparable plywood product.

But Georgia-Pacific was not ready to give up. Pamplin intended to conduct a secret experiment in plywood production that went against the accepted wisdom of the entire industry. He turned to one of the company's most colorful managers, Jens Jorgensen, general manager of G-P's Northwest plywood plants. Jorgensen had joined Georgia-Pacific through the

Coos Bay Lumber Co. acquisition. Jorgensen had a third-grade education and could neither compose a business letter nor speak with correct grammar. He delighted in firing anyone with a college education, but he had a reputation for letting the managers below him make changes to develop better products and manufacturing techniques.

Jorgensen led the Southern pine plywood operation, which was conducted with military-type secrecy. The first step, recalls Davis Mortensen, was to ship Crossett pine logs to Savannah, where Georgia-Pacific had a hardwood plywood operation.

"We sent the logs to Savannah and they peeled them and dried the veneer and laid it up and sent the panels back to Crossett. I remember the day that a group of people came to look at that plywood," Mortensen says. "The plywood looked horrible. It was bowed, crooked. It just looked terrible. I remember Jens Jorgensen saying, 'This is going to be good.' He intuitively knew that this beginning was good enough, that if we kept going we could eventually turn out a better product. It turned out to be a fantastic product."

G-P continued the process, now sending pine logs to the West Coast plywood operations, where experiments were conducted in peeling the pine and gluing the layers of veneer. John Rasor, who later became executive vice president of wood procurement, gypsum and industrial wood products, was driving a lift truck at the Springfield, Oregon, complex when the pine logs began to arrive on the West Coast.

"The rotary peeling was the first issue," Rasor recalls. "But probably equal, if not more challenging,

The Southern pine plywood operation was conducted with military-type secrecy. "We worked harder at it and smarter at it than anybody else."

Georgia-Pacific's pioneering work with Southern pine quickly found effective uses for these trees. The shipment above is the first truckload of Southern pine particleboard produced at a new plant in Taylorsville, Mississippi, one of many plants to pop up around the South during G-P's wave of expansion in the 1960s.

was the development of an adhesive system that would give you the kind of bond that you needed to ensure the integrity of the panel and its performance in the field."

The other challenge was the timing. Other companies, including Temple-Inland were working on similar projects, and the G-P team knew the first product to market would have the advantage. "We worked harder at it and smarter at it than anybody else," Rasor says.

Back in Arkansas, G-P bet heavily on this experiment. Soon after it acquired Fordyce Lumber

Company, G-P closed the sawmill and built a plywood mill. "They got it built and started making plywood, then they started learning how to make it better," recalls Davis Mortensen. "They started off heating the logs in steam chests to prepare them for peeling. That didn't work real well. Eventually, they learned to use vats filled with hot water."

The next piece of the puzzle was the glue. "The theory was that the glue wouldn't hold Southern pine plywood," says Stanley Dennison, who was head of G-P's Southern region at the time. "Indeed, that was true if you used interior glue, which most plywood was made with at that time, including Western plywood. G-P mixed exterior and interior glue half-and-half, and that improved it tremendously, but it was still delaminating. Then, in a meeting in Oregon, they decided to go for all exterior-grade glue, and that solved the problem."

Georgia-Pacific had created a viable process to manufacture Southern pine plywood.

GROWTH SPURT

"That breakthrough had a fantastic, overriding effect on Georgia-Pacific, first in the South and then in a lot of other parts of the country," Dennison says. "It was primarily a Southern product. Previously, they used very little plywood in homebuilding in the South. They only had used Western plywood for boat panels and decorative uses." Freight rates were high for Western plywood and Southern builders preferred one-by-six boards to plywood sheathing.

Now that Georgia-Pacific had created the new product, the task fell to Dennison to sell it in the Southern region, where he oversaw three distribution centers, in Atlanta, Miami and Mobile, Alabama. "My biggest job was convincing the builders to use plywood," Dennison says. "I wasn't even selling directly to the builders, but to the dealers. I had to get the builders interested in using the product. So, if a builder had five houses going up, I would work with a dealer to give the builder one house of plywood free if he used plywood on all five.

"We started doing some advertising, but the most powerful argument was giving the builders stopwatch timing on the labor it took to roof a house with one-by-six — including unloading it from the truck up to the house and finishing off the roof — against using a four-by-eight plywood panel. Of course, with the plywood it took about half the time and labor. That did a lot toward convincing them."

Pamplin quickly moved in on the opportunity he had foreseen, and Georgia-Pacific embarked on the most extensive period of expansion in its history. Flowerree credits Pamplin with the ingenuity and vision to press for the process to manufacture Southern pine plywood. "That created a whole new industry, really," he says. "We had a plywood plant behind every stump. It led to an amazing amount of growth."

"Demand just skyrocketed," Mortensen says. "We built plywood plants all over the Southeast." John Rasor recalls that the company's ambition was almost without limit: to have a plywood plant and a lumber operation "everywhere the opportunity presented itself across the Southern pine belt" from East Texas to the Atlantic Coast. "It was more than just a strategic plan," he says. "There were times that we were building two and three mills at the same time."

Georgia-Pacific began building "chip-n-saw" mills, which Rasor describes as midsize lumber sawmill operations designed to take advantage of the size of logs growing in the Southern pine forests and pulpwood plantations. Smaller logs were typically chipped up to make pulp, while larger diameter timber was used for conventional saw milling and plywood. G-P's

timber holdings in the South often produced logs that were "halfway between chips and saw." The versatile mills G-P built produced both chips and saw timber and enabled the company to produce two products with the capital expenditure formerly required to produce one.

In 1967, Pamplin succeeded Cheatham as chairman of the board. Cheatham, who retired at the company's mandatory age of 65, remained on the board as a director and as honorary chairman. Pamplin, surrounded by four talented executive vice presidents — Flowerree, Kane, William Hunt and Julian Cheatham — led Georgia-Pacific to sales of more than $1 billion in 1968.

Sales increases were facilitated by the company's strong distribution system. "The distribution division

The company's hardwood plywood operation in Savannah, above, played a critical role in the development of Southern pine plywood. It was here that the first Southern pine logs were, peeled, layered and glued. At left, sheets of hardwood veneer await transport from this Savannah warehouse to the port for shipping.

could sell anything," Flowerree says. "It helped our plywood plants tremendously." With the constant drumbeat of sales, G-P was able to keep its plywood plants running. "Champion and U.S. Plywood people told me they didn't know how we ran those plants so well. We were way below the cost of anybody else. And part of the secret was that the distribution division was selling the plywood as fast as we could make it," Flowerree says.

Pamplin and Hunt had guaranteed a steady supply of gypsum wallboard for the distribution division with the 1965 acquisition of Bestwall Gypsum Company of Paoli, Pennsylvania, which previously had been a supplier to G-P. By 1965, G-P had 84 distribution centers. The centers, like every other facet of G-P, were decentralized and reflected the leadership of the local manager. A manager had the flexibility to tailor his center to the local market.

In 1970, Dennison was named vice president of the division and moved to Portland. Harold Sand, who had joined G-P in 1956 when the company acquired his family business, Charles E. Sand Plywood Company, moved up to executive vice president. Under Sand and Dennison, the division became a profit center for the company. Dennison located new centers by studying demographic and economic information. Once a center generated $200,000 in sales a month, Dennison immediately began looking to locate a new center in a promising territory nearby.

"All states were measured that way," Dennison recalls. "We took housing starts, population growth and growth of wealth into consideration."

Georgia-Pacific acquired Bestwall Gypsum Company in 1965 to guarantee a steady supply of gypsum wallboard for the distribution division. G-P now has both underground gypsum mines, left, and quarries, with extensive reserves for future needs. The company uses gypsum to make wallboard, specialty panels, fire-door cores, industrial plaster and joint compound.

Georgia-Pacific originally produced resins to supply its own wood products manufacturing facilities, but later became the industry's leading supplier of wood resins, pine chemicals and specialty chemicals. The Chemical Research Facility at Decatur, Georgia, above and right, develops new uses for wood-based chemicals. The company produces thermosetting resins, pulp and paper chemicals, chemicals derived from lignin (the natural glue that holds wood fibers together), and tall oil, which provides many end-use options.

THE MOVE INTO CHEMICALS

To cope with the growth that integration was bringing, Flowerree created an engineering department to design and build new facilities. In 1964, Flowerree created a chemicals division at Bellingham and put Eric Ericsson, a chemical engineer, in charge. At Bellingham, G-P built a chlorine and caustic soda plant, followed shortly afterward by a sodium chlorate and sulfuric acid plant.

The company extended its chemical expertise into the manufacture of the resins needed as adhesives for both plywood and hardwood plants. Georgia-Pacific's chemical business began in 1959 with the start-up of a phenolic resin adhesive plant in Coos Bay, Oregon, to supply the company's wood products operations on the West Coast. The chlorine and caustic soda produced at Bellingham were used in the manufacturing process at the Bellingham and Samoa, California, operations as well as the Ketchikan, Alaska, pulp mill. In addition, G-P produced lignin products for sale to industry and agriculture, including uses in cement, drilling muds and fertilizer.

Flowerree also rounded out the company's product lines in paper. He oversaw the acquisition in 1965 of George La Monte & Son of Nutley, New Jersey, which manufactured safety paper for banks and other businesses, and in 1967 of Kalamazoo Paper Company, which manufactured coated paper.

In 1966, G-P built a chip facility at Coos Bay and began to export chips to Japan, which was becoming a prime customer, not only for chips, but also for logs and pulp. Pamplin negotiated directly with representatives of Japanese trading companies, such as C. Itoh and Marubeni, who were impressed that a top executive would deal with them directly. The same year, Georgia-Pacific expanded its chemical business, acquiring chemical facilities from National Polychemicals, Inc., in Lufkin, Texas, and Conway, North Carolina.

To produce the raw materials for resins needed by the company, Flowerree turned his attention to his native Louisiana, where a petrochemical industry had grown up along the Mississippi River and the Texas Gulf Coast. Flowerree purchased a former sugar cane plantation known as "Rebecca" near the small town of Plaquemine, Louisiana, where G-P began construction in 1968 of a complex to manufacture phenol and methanol.

The community agreed to raise $75 million through Louisiana Industrial Revenue Bonds to finance the project. G-P agreed not to take any of the money down until the company completed the project, which proved to be a mistake. G-P had so many other projects underway at the time that Kane needed to raise the $75 million from outside sources. He found a credit organization that seemed willing to lend the funds and went to Dallas to meet with a lender's representative. The rep drove up in a white Cadillac with gold interior and agreed to lend the money if his company could co-sign for the plant. Kane suspected the man might have underworld ties and rushed back to Portland.

Kane called Jimmy Miller of Blyth, Eastman & Dillon & Company at 3 a.m. the next morning and,

Georgia-Pacific broke ground on its new headquarters building in 1967 and celebrated the grand opening of the building in 1970. The tallest building in Portland, opposite, the new G-P headquarters featured a controversial nude statue, obscured in the picture at right by the young men and women helping to celebrate the grand opening.

through him, was able to sell $75 million in convertible debentures. The chemical complex continued to rise.

G-P produced more chemicals than its manufacturing operations could use and Flowerree created a chemical sales division in 1967 to sell the surplus. James R. Kuse, a Union Carbide veteran who joined G-P in 1968, was eventually named head of chemical sales.

Although Georgia-Pacific had encountered resentment and resistance when it moved into the Northwest, it was welcomed with open arms in the South. When Georgia-Pacific built an operation in a Southern town it almost always became the employer of choice, with the best job opportunities in the community. In Oregon, the company typically bought

an existing property and sometimes closed or sold off some of its operations. In the South in the 1960s, G-P was opening up completely new opportunities.

Pamplin delivered a speech in Arkansas in which he noted that G-P returned to the South because of opportunities to buy timberlands. And as soon as the company worked out the process of making plywood from Southern pine, it "pushed across the South creating a dynamic new industry and possibly saving the plywood industry," according to *Maverick*.

Georgia-Pacific's operations were now spread across the country and quite heavily concentrated along the Southern pine belt. Nevertheless, in 1970, the company opened a dramatic new headquarters

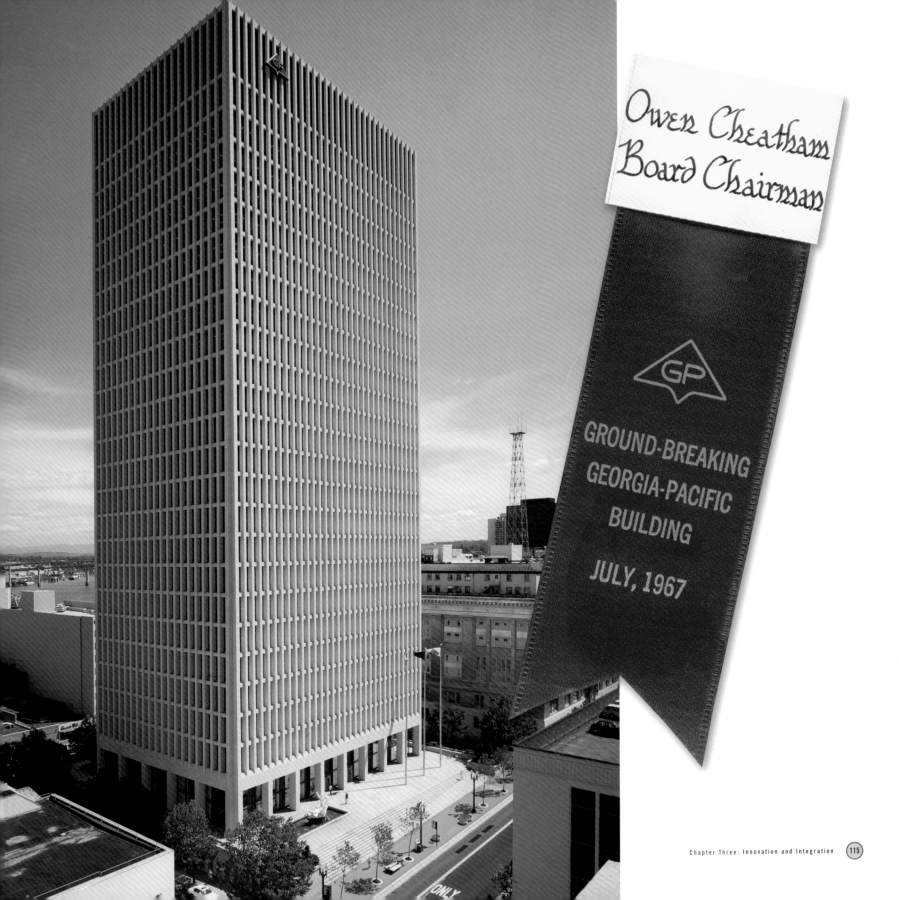

Owen Cheatham
Board Chairman

GP

GROUND-BREAKING
GEORGIA-PACIFIC
BUILDING

JULY, 1967

Robert Pamplin (left) and Owen Cheatham cut the cake celebrating the opening of Georgia-Pacific's 100th distribution center. The centers were instrumental in the company's rapid growth in the 1960s. As Robert Flowerree put it, "The distribution division could sell anything."

building in downtown Portland, seemingly reinforcing its commitment to the Pacific Northwest.

THE PARTY'S OVER

While Georgia-Pacific may have been welcomed warmly by the small Southern communities it revitalized, the company's dramatic thrust across the South with Southern pine plywood raised the ire of competitors and caught the attention of the Federal Trade Commission (FTC). In June 1971, the FTC challenged G-P's market position for the manufacture of Southern pine plywood and ownership of Southern timberlands, alleging that the company's position could lessen competition or tend to create a monopoly in the softwood plywood industry.

The FTC action came on the heels of complaints from the Southeastern Lumbermen's Association and a group of 10 Savannah River Basin lumbermen, small sawmills that blamed G-P for their slacking business. At the time, G-P's operations, as well as those of St. Regis, Weyerhaeuser, Willamette Industries and others, had created such a demand for timber that the prices skyrocketed, making it difficult for small sawmills to stay in the business. The lumbermen wanted a chance to buy the new plywood plants that G-P had built at a favorable price. The FTC wanted Georgia-Pacific to divest certain timberlands and eight plywood plants in the South.

Thirty years later, Bob Flowerree compared the government's action to the case against Microsoft in the late 1990s. "There wasn't anything to it,"

Flowerree says. "We were wrongly accused. Anybody gets successful, like Bill Gates, and they take out after him. They haven't changed; it's just a different bunch."

While G-P had pioneered Southern pine plywood, other companies had jumped into the market. Georgia-Pacific owned only one third of the plants that manufactured plywood. Furthermore, Pamplin believed the development of Southern pine plywood saved customers from the trauma of short supply and high prices. Douglas fir did not grow rapidly enough to keep up with the demand for plywood. At one point, Pamplin wrote a letter to President Richard Nixon asking why the government was trying to make an efficient organization subsidize the less efficient. But the case lingered.

Georgia-Pacific's legal staff reported to Pamplin that of approximately 200 cases involving the FTC, the federal agency had lost only one. Pamplin saw little reason to waste corporate funds fighting the agency and damaging the corporate image. So he and his fellow officers came up with a novel solution to the complaint. He proposed to spin off part of G-P's assets and properties as a new corporation. The FTC agreed.

As a result, the Louisiana-Pacific Corporation was created with $305 million in assets, including the plywood plants and sawmills in Louisiana and Texas; the redwood and pulp operations in Samoa, California; the redwood forest and lumber operations at Ukiah, California; the Intermountain operations in eastern Oregon, Washington and Idaho; the pulp and lumber operations in Ketchikan, Alaska; and a window and door operation in Barberton, Ohio.

The solution saved most of Georgia-Pacific's Southern pine plywood plants. For stockholders, the spin-off provided a bonus — a 1-for-4 stock split. G-P and L-P were two forest products giants with essentially the same shareholders.

William Hunt was named chairman of Louisiana-Pacific and Pamplin named Harry Merlo, an aggressive entrepreneur considered by some G-P insiders too ambitious for their liking, to be L-P's president and chief executive officer. Merlo had been introduced to the company through Julian Cheatham, and had run the Samoa division in California as if it were his own.

"Harry Merlo was quite a promoter and a good operator," Flowerree recalls. "He was his own man, as everybody at G-P in those days was."

After the FTC accepted the arrangement, Boise Cascade, which was having financial troubles at the time, offered G-P its Fort Bragg, California, redwood mill, a beautiful facility on the Pacific Ocean. The FTC approved and Pamplin and Kane arranged a deal, with G-P taking 187,821 acres of redwood timberlands and Louisiana-Pacific taking approximately 50,000 acres for its Ukiah division. The plywood plant went to L-P.

After Georgia-Pacific put the FTC action behind it, the company continued its aggressive ways by announcing in 1973 a $1 billion, five-year capital investment program. By that year, sales had reached $2.2 billion.

As Georgia-Pacific moved into the mid-1970s, Robert B. Pamplin was thinking about bringing his

remarkable career at the company to a close. But he wasn't slowing down, as Stanley Dennison recalls.

"Bob Pamplin was a very outspoken man," he says. "David Rockefeller used to come out once a year from Chase Manhattan Bank. Rockefeller was going on and on about how businesses should be run and how bankers relate to business. At that time, interest rates were pretty high. And Bob Pamplin says, 'The big problem with you guys is you don't know when to lower interest rates so people can do business with you!'"

As one of Georgia-Pacific's guiding lights for three decades and after leading it through its most prosperous years of growth, Pamplin was preparing to retire in name only. He had already prepared himself for a second career that would last almost as long and would be every bit as remarkable as the first.

Georgia-Pacific's success with Southern pine plywood eventually drew the attention of the Federal Trade Commission. When Georgia-Pacific spun off Louisiana-Pacific in 1972, it gave up Western plywood operations that G-P had been running for decades, below, in order to keep its highly profitable Southern plywood plants. Louisiana-Pacific today owns almost a million acres of timberland and runs more than 60 manufacturing facilities.

You Can

Go Home

Again

W hen the day finally arrived for Bob Pamplin to retire, "he just got up and left," recalls former treasurer Marion Talmadge. On November 30, 1976, without pomp of any kind, Pamplin simply turned over the reins of the company he had forged into one of America's great growth engines and walked out of the headquarters building at Fifth and Taylor into the crisp Portland air. Pamplin's final year at the Georgia-Pacific helm concluded five successive five-year periods in which G-P had doubled earnings. When Pamplin became president of the company in 1957, net income was $7.4 million on sales of $121 million. For 1976, G-P's net income was $215.3 million on sales of $4.038 billion, signifying Pamplin's term as one of the most remarkable performances by a corporate leader in the history of American industry.

Pamplin's departure put Georgia-Pacific in the hands of his designated successor, Bob Flowerree, who had long guided the company's operations. Pamplin had named Flowerree president in 1975, as Flowerree already had made enormous contributions to G-P, particularly in integrating and diversifying the company into chemicals, paper and tissue and in driving G-P's effort to be the industry's low-cost producer. The diversification helped strengthen the company overall to cope with the cycles of the up-and-down industry.

Although Flowerree had played a critical role in building G-P alongside Pamplin, he had never given thought to becoming chairman of G-P. "I was too busy working to think of that," he says. "We worked seven days a week just about. I was traveling all the time and had so much responsibility that I didn't have time to think about those kinds of things. It was a very thin operation. You did everything yourself. You didn't hire any consultants. If you had to hire a consultant, Bob would figure you didn't know your job and he'd fire you."

It was Pamplin's leadership style to turn over responsibility to his management team and expect them to handle it without supervision, and in this environment, Flowerree developed into a capable leader. In later years, Flowerree continued to praise Pamplin as a genius: "He was very astute and an outstanding leader, and the morale was just excellent. When I became chairman, I was honored. I had pretty big shoes to fill."

As logical as Flowerree's succession to the chairmanship might have been, Pamplin did not turn over to him the complete leadership package. Pamplin designated Marshall Hahn to serve as president under Flowerree. In fact, in the early 1970s, Pamplin had entertained the idea of training Hahn as his successor to the chairmanship.

Hahn was a fellow Southerner with a rustic Kentucky twang in his voice that belied his Ph.D. in physics from the Massachusetts Institute of Technology. He became president of Virginia Polytechnic Institute at the tender age of 35 and was as cocky as a rooster, in sharp contrast to the more genteel Flowerree. Hahn was so respected as a strong college administrator that he was touted as a possible candidate for governor of Virginia in 1969.

While serving as Tech's president, Hahn had traveled to Oregon and raised substantial gifts from both Pamplin and Julian Cheatham, who had roomed together at Virginia Tech. As a result, the Blacksburg, Virginia, campus today is graced by both Pamplin Hall and Cheatham Hall. In Hahn, the leather-tough Pamplin could see a younger version of himself.

When Pamplin was about five years from retirement, he began trying to recruit Hahn, "I knew he had done an outstanding job at Virginia Tech and he was a tough person," Pamplin said in an interview for a company video. "He ran things pretty well back there, and I thought that maybe he could do it here."

Hahn originally agreed to go west, but backed out because his wife didn't want to move. Two years later, Hahn changed his mind. He moved to Portland in 1975 to take over the chemical division, but Pamplin knew Hahn would not be prepared to succeed him as chairman a year later. "His time was too short," Pamplin said in the video. "He couldn't prove himself in that period of time."

When Pamplin decided to retire, the chairman examined his options. "That's when I decided Bob Flowerree was ready for the top job," Pamplin explains.

BOLD STEPS

"Pamplin didn't do much in the way of training Bob Flowerree for all the different things he was taking over," says Marion Talmadge. But Flowerree moved ahead with confidence, continuing to acquire companies, build new operations and increase sales. As an operations man, he dutifully followed in the style set by Pamplin, "Bob [Flowerree] was a very low-key guy," says Steve Jackson. "No secrets. No pretentiousness. He carried forward the Pamplin ethic: head-down, ass-up, work hard. No frills. No nonsense."

As an example of Flowerree's plainspoken approach to business, Jackson recalls the story of a mill accountant who complained to Flowerree that an hourly employee running a winder was making more money than the accountants. Flowerree replied matter-of-factly, "Why don't you get a job working on the winder?"

But in some aspects, Flowerree's management style diverged sharply from his predecessor's. One notable difference was that Flowerree ran the company more through consensus. In *Maverick*, author John Ross notes that the Operating Policy Committee meetings,

Bob Pamplin didn't exactly retire in 1976, when he left Georgia-Pacific. He simply took over the chairmanship of his own company, R. B. Pamplin Corporation, and continued doing business for nearly another quarter-century. He acquired and operated a group of companies in a range of industries, including textiles and communications.

His son, Dr. Robert B. Pamplin Jr., joined him in the business and became widely known not only as a businessman, but also as a minister, philanthropist, author, teacher and political activist. Both father and son contributed enormous sums of money to charity. Driving the Pamplins' success, as well as their philanthropy, was a devotion to the bedrock conservative values that the senior Pamplin had brought with him out of Virginia in the early days of the twentieth century.

Pamplin Jr. wrote a loving biography of his father in 1986 titled *Another Virginian: A Study of the Life and Beliefs of Robert Boisseau Pamplin.* In it, the son described the shrewd fashion in which his father set up his own company:

The senior Pamplin organized R. B. Pamplin Corp. in 1957, placing 20,000 shares of Georgia-Pacific common stock in the company for 100 percent of its capital stock and borrowing money from a bank to purchase real estate, with income from the real estate equal to 50 percent or more of the dividends received from the G-P stock. "This prevented the company from being a personal holding company, and as a result the dividends from Georgia-Pacific common stock were considered 85 percent

tax exempt," Pamplin Jr. wrote.

Pamplin used the same creative financing in his own company that he had developed to build Georgia-Pacific. Steve Jackson recalls a saying about Pamplin's method of buying companies: "He bought it on a dime — the dime he had to borrow to make a phone call to get the money." The bottom line of the Pamplin strategy, Jackson says, was that "he got all his companies without cash."

Pamplin's favorite formula — both at G-P and at Pamplin Corp. — was to sell a piece of the acquired business to pay for the purchase. After Pamplin left G-P, Jackson recalls, "he bought a sand and gravel company in Portland [Ross Island]. When he went out to look at it, there were all these trucks standing around the parking lot. He asked, 'When do these trucks go out and do their business?' And they said, 'Oh, these are extra trucks.' So he bought the company and sold the extra trucks."

A few years later, Pamplin bought a diaper company that had both a paper business and a cloth business, and Georgia-Pacific ended up on the other side of Pamplin's familiar tactic. Jackson recalls the feeling as Pamplin convinced G-P to buy the paper diaper business: "It was like, 'Wait! Stop! Don't you realize what he's doing? He's sticking us with that diaper business!'"

The strategy worked as well for R. B. Pamplin Corp. as it had for G-P. By 1999, Pamplin's corporation was ranked 266th on the Forbes 500 list of America's largest private companies with sales of $800 million.

Pamplin attended his retirement party in 1976 and immediately took over the chairmanship of his own company, R. B. Pamplin Corporation, which had sales of $800 million in 1999. Pamplin split with Georgia-Pacific in the late 1970s over changes in the retirement plan for executive officers.

the traditional Monday breakfasts and the company's standards review were more like forums than hearings, and "officers at every level breathed easier." Flowerree brought in new talent in advertising and public relations, traffic and engineering. He created an office in Portland for a vice president of timberlands and replaced the stock dividend with a cash dividend.

Flowerree's consensus approach did not include Pamplin, however. Flowerree formulated his new policies and presented them to the board of directors for approval without discussing them with Pamplin beforehand. This upset Pamplin, who not only served on the board, but also had a consulting agreement with the company.

Ultimately, Flowerree took bold steps that made it clear the Pamplin era was over. First, he backed a wholesale change in the company's retirement plan for salaried employees, allowing them to expand their retirement investment opportunities beyond G-P's Stock Bonus Plan pension. The traditional plan put 10 percent of an employee's salary in G-P stock. In the years when the stock boomed, the plan was far superior to its modern equivalents. But Flowerree noted that by the late 1970s, times had changed.

"After the company matured, you didn't get that growth you had in the early days, so we had to change the pension plan," Flowerree says. "Bob [Pamplin] didn't want to change it, but it wasn't competitive. We couldn't hire anybody. Some people were even considering leaving the company because of it. It just wasn't adequate any longer."

Talmadge, who administered the plan, recalls,

"We felt it was too restrictive, that it should have the potential of growth in other stocks."

As CEO, Flowerree instituted a straightforward salary and service formula, broadening the investment options beyond G-P stock. The change — and the fact that it was instituted against Pamplin's wishes and without his input — so infuriated the former chairman that he resigned from the board of directors in January 1978. Pamplin reflected the depth of his hurt in a 1979 series about Georgia-Pacific in the alternative weekly newspaper *Willamette Week* by writer Anthony Bianco.

"I've been with the company a long time and was largely responsible for building the company, and then they don't want to hear from me," Pamplin said. "On something as important as the pension, they don't want to listen to me. To me, it's just inconceivable.... I don't know how to explain it."

But the pension plan change was nothing compared with what came next.

SURPRISE ANNOUNCEMENT

In October 1978, Bob Flowerree shocked the entire state of Oregon when Georgia-Pacific announced it was moving back to the South.

Steve Jackson, who was vice president of advertising and public relations at the time, recalls that the announcement was hurried and purely reactive. The company was already deep in negotiations for a building site in downtown Atlanta, but G-P executives had intended to withhold the announcement until the deal was finalized. However, the closely held secret was leaked by an unknown party to the *Atlanta Constitution*. Once the story broke in Atlanta, Jackson and the company's executives scrambled to tell the employees before the Portland media could beat them to it.

"We called all of the employees into the auditorium, and we announced we were moving the headquarters somewhere in the Southeast. Then we had a press conference to tell the media we were moving. The first meeting and the press conference were held quickly because the story was going to break in the evening paper," Jackson recalls. "Then we held another meeting with employees the next day to answer questions they had. But because we were caught by surprise, there were many questions we did not have the answers to. We were going to move in four years and had not started to plan yet. The real estate deal had just gone through. That is what triggered the story in the first place."

Georgia-Pacific executives had some explaining to do about the timing of the announcement, but they insisted that the move was necessary because the bulk of G-P's business was now in the South, following the runaway success of Southern pine plywood and the spin-off of Louisiana-Pacific, with properties that were mostly in the West. By the late 1970s, roughly three-fourths of G-P's income and profits were generated east of the Mississippi River. "We simply realized we were running a Southeastern company from the Pacific Northwest," Steve Jackson says.

In addition, the environmental movement was

gaining momentum in Oregon, which was becoming palpably less hospitable for an aggressive wood products company, even if it was the largest business in the state. Oregon's tax rates were higher than Georgia's. Furthermore, in the Northwest, the federal government controlled most of the forests, whereas timber ownership in the South was heavily in the hands of private owners.

Pamplin told *Willamette Week* in 1979 that he had briefly considered moving G-P to the South in 1974 but decided to stay in Portland to avoid a mass defection of talent. "You're talking about an awful lot of people — good people," Pamplin said. "I knew a lot of them wouldn't move. It would have done more harm than good attempting it." But just four years after Pamplin considered and rejected a move, Flowerree and the board made the decision to leave

In 1978, Georgia-Pacific shocked Portland by announcing it was moving its headquarters back to the South. Robert Flowerree said the impetus for the move was the Louisiana-Pacific spin-off. G-P set up an information room in Portland to explain the move and the destination, Atlanta, to employees — some of whom were afraid of Georgia's poisonous snakes! G-P even offered generous mortgage rates to encourage its headquarters employees to make the move. Approximately half of the 400 employees did.

Georgia-Pacific chose a building site in the heart of downtown Atlanta and immediately stirred up local controversy when it dismantled this treasured old Coca-Cola sign, above. The G-P site had once included the historic Loew's Grand Theatre, opposite, which had hosted the premier of the movie *Gone With the Wind*. The theater was destroyed by fire at the time the company was scouting for locations, but Georgia-Pacific donated a piece of land that the city converted into Margaret Mitchell Square to honor the author of the classic Southern novel.

Portland and return to G-P's roots in the Southeast.

"It was strictly a business decision," Flowerree says. "I think the real impetus was the Louisiana-Pacific spin-off." He jokes that the company's frequent coast-to-coast trips were supporting United Airlines. Indeed, the skies were filled with commercial and company planes ferrying executives on long journeys between G-P's Portland headquarters and its major markets and plants in the Southeast. It was on one such flight, the story goes, that the plan to move really came together. "Bob Flowerree was in a company airplane flying across the country. He got over Atlanta and said, 'This is where we're going to move,'" Talmadge recalls.

Perhaps it was Atlanta's inviting canopy of trees that caught Flowerree's attention. More likely, it was Atlanta's convenient location as the commercial hub of the South and its busy Hartsfield International Airport, which had direct flights to places like Baton Rouge, Louisiana, and other G-P locations. Steve Jackson estimated the move back to the South would save the company as much as $3 million a year in travel expenses and another $3 million in executive time.

Although the reasoning behind the decision was sound, the Portland business community was shocked and angered that Oregon's largest corporation would pull up stakes and leave, raising the old specter of G-P as a "cut and run" company. But Flowerree believed that Oregon wasn't as sympathetic to business as Georgia. He told the Atlanta news conference announcing G-P's move: "In the West when you announce something like this, people say, 'Why are you bringing all those jobs here? You're

ruining the hunting and fishing.'"

The business community had glimpsed what was coming in February 1978 when G-P said it was moving its 40-person central engineering staff from Portland to Atlanta, where it would be closer to the plants it was designing. "That was the big blow to Portland," Oliver Larson, president of the Portland Chamber of Commerce at the time, told *Willamette Week*. "In my opinion, that was when the deed was done. The chamber was screaming blue apples in February. I went stomping over there and raising hell. But from that point on I got nothing but PR pablum. By the time the October announcement came, we were resigned to their loss."

After the announcement, Larson told *Business Week*, "We feel demolished and impoverished. We don't ask anyone to come here, but we are as insulted as hell when they leave." More than one Portland official suggested impolitely that when G-P moved, the company should take with it the controversial nude statue in front of its building. Mayor Neil Goldschmidt belittled G-P's past contribution to Portland in the *Oregonian*, saying, "I don't see this having a significant effect on the city's economy." He later wrote a letter to Flowerree apologizing and acknowledging G-P's historic role as a "stalwart leader" in civic affairs.

Flowerree admitted that the reaction affected him deeply, but he never doubted the wisdom of the move. "The natives around Portland ostracized me like you wouldn't believe," he recalls. "But if we had to do it again, I'd make the same decision."

Jack Samper, the G-P executive who headed the move, had to fight the many negative images about the South that had lodged in the minds of some G-P employees. "The South has kind of an interesting reputation," he told the *Constitution*. "When you think of the South, you think of stereotypes: hot in the summer — when no one works — riots periodically, crime is rampant, bugs come in and eat you in your home."

Walter Cheatham, nephew of Owen and Julian and the last member of the family to work for G-P, joined the company in 1975 and transferred to Portland when the move was announced to help ease the transition. Cheatham, who worked for Samper, recalls a far-fetched story exemplifying the stereotypes that fed employees' fears. "One woman came to Jack and said she didn't want to move to Atlanta," Cheatham recalls. "She liked living in Oregon and she loved water skiing and wanted to stay there. Jack said, 'Well, it strikes me that water skiing will be much better in Georgia. They have a much longer season. You've got two or three big lakes.' And she said, 'No, it's dangerous to ski in the South. When the water moccasins hear the boats, they line up on the shore to go after whoever falls.' She was serious. That was the craziest story I ever heard."

Cheatham was involved with a group in G-P's Portland office called the Atlanta Club, which the company organized as a way to dispel these notions, promote the move and answer employee questions about the new headquarters city. Realtors and bankers from Atlanta flew out to speak to the group, which staged parties and a mountain climbing expedition to the top of Mount Hood. The club set up a room

called "123 Peachtree Street," the supposed address of the new headquarters building, which ultimately became 133 Peachtree Street.

G-P went to great lengths to persuade employees to move across the country to an unknown city that had gotten bad press. "We quickly had to put together a four-year plan on how to convince people to go," says Steve Jackson. "Everybody who expressed an interest was flown to Atlanta and we showed them the town. It was probably the most dramatic thing I've ever done in my life."

To make the move as attractive as possible, G-P offered employees an extraordinary mortgage deal — 8.5 percent interest. The offer later would prove to have extremely damaging consequences to the company's bottom line at a time it could ill-afford such generosity.

Ultimately, of the 400 headquarters employees, approximately half decided to move to Atlanta. The other half left G-P to remain in Portland. Jackson notes that after all the company's efforts, it motivated 50 percent of the eligible workforce to take the transfer, which was the national average for such moves.

G-P also decided to close its long-time Augusta, Georgia, office and move that staff to Atlanta as well. Like Portland, Augusta, the company's birthplace, was deeply wounded by the decision.

THE ECONOMY TURNS

After the firestorm of controversy about the move subsided, Flowerree settled into what had become a routine of successful years at G-P. Each of his first three years as chairman and CEO was better than the last, and by 1979, net income had reached $327 million on sales of $5.2 billion.

Flowerree had started out with a roar, but trouble was brewing in the building products sector, which was seeing depressed prices and increased raw material costs. The dark cloud of an economic slowdown cast an ominous shadow over much of the nation. Yet G-P kept buying businesses: Hudson Pulp and Paper Corp., which added 550,000 acres of timberland, mostly in Florida; BRK Petroleum, Inc., with natural gas reserves; and Polymer Materials, Inc., a diversified supplier to the plastics industry.

In 1979, the company sold $150 million of floating interest rate notes, following the strategy of Chief Financial Officer Harry Kane. It seemed to make sense at the time. After all, the logic went, how much higher could the rates go above the initial rate of 8.5 percent? The company would soon find out that the rates could go much, much higher. A tidal wave of inflation was headed for the American economy.

The company's debt reached $1.05 billion in 1979, nearly 40 percent more than the year before. But the dangers of inflation, though visible on the horizon, were still too far off to dim the warm glow of national publicity about G-P's accomplishments of the preceding quarter-century.

In 1980, *Fortune* magazine revisited the first 25 years of its Fortune 500 rankings and pointed out that Georgia-Pacific had one of the most remarkable growth records in the nation during that period. From 1954 through 1979, G-P was ranked second in sales growth (19.2 percent), ranked second in earnings per share growth (18 percent), tied for fifth in the increase in jobs (10.5 percent) and ranked fourth in stock performance — $100 invested in G-P stock in 1954 was worth $6,056 in 1979. For comparison, IBM was ranked sixth in sales growth and fifth in EPS growth. And G-P's spin-off, Louisiana-Pacific, was ranked among the 30 youngest Fortune 500 companies. L-P was number 236 overall as a seven-year-old enterprise with sales of $1.3 billion. G-P was ranked number 56 overall on the 1980 list.

Fortune noted G-P had been among America's "most voracious acquirers" of new companies in the preceding quarter-century. "Georgia-Pacific — the company that ranks No. 2 in sales growth — has made about 70 acquisitions over the years — transforming itself along the way from a relatively small lumber company into a fully integrated pulp and paper manufacturer," the magazine wrote.

That same issue of *Fortune* noted ominously that in 1979, corporations were "fearing recession and encountering the most virulent inflation in thirty-two years."

Indeed, in 1980, the wheels began to come off the national economy and G-P felt the heat. The economy was in such rough shape — as inflation reached a frightening 18 percent — that Ronald Reagan was able to wrest the presidency from incumbent Jimmy Carter by asking voters a simple question, "Are you better off than you were four years ago?"

Double-digit mortgage rates hammered the

The new Georgia-Pacific building made a dramatic entrance on the Atlanta skyline during the recession of the early 1980s. Covered with sunset-colored granite, the 52-story skyscraper swept upward like a giant redwood, opposite. Art permeates the building, including the downtown branch of Atlanta's High Museum of Art, which is housed there. Marshall Hahn, who joined Georgia-Pacific in Portland and made the move South, championed the work of local, self-taught artist Mattie Lou O'Kelley, whose work, above, is still displayed at G-P headquarters and in Hahn's nationally recognized collection of primitive art.

THE PINK PALACE

For its new headquarters in downtown Atlanta, Georgia-Pacific built a stunning 52-story building with an exterior of "sunset red" granite, which was more like a dusky pink. Employees quickly nicknamed it "the Pink Palace." Atlanta newspapers stirred controversy about a pink building going up downtown, but the color turned out to be much more subtle than critics feared.

Designed by Belgian-born architect Leon Moed of the architectural firm Skidmore, Owings & Merrill, the tower was built at a cost of $90 million. The building is terraced at 11-story intervals. Its west façade, facing Peachtree Street, slants slightly back to the east, giving the building the strong sense of sweeping powerfully upward. It towers over the sidewalk like a giant redwood and glows with a remarkable reflection as the sun sets each evening.

The building has had an impressive impact on customers, according to Steve Jackson. As vice president of the distribution division, he recalls clients who would marvel at the skyscraper rising boldly above Peachtree Street and exclaim, "Wow! I didn't realize I was working with such a big company!"

The building and its location were widely praised as a pioneering step in the revitalization of downtown Atlanta. G-P was credited in Atlanta for having the courage to reinvigorate the downtown area at a time when many people, including the national media, had written it off.

Asked years later why G-P decided to locate downtown despite the controversy about the inner city, former chairman Bob Flowerree said, "It was a tradition in the company. Owen Cheatham always liked to be downtown. He

was in downtown New York. We were in downtown Portland. With the subway coming at that time, we thought it would be easy to get people back and forth. We just thought it made a lot of sense."

The building replaced several Atlanta icons, notably the Loew's Grand Theatre, which earlier was destroyed by fire. The headquarters' construction also led G-P to ask the Coca-Cola Co. to remove one of Atlanta's most recognizable landmarks, a huge circular neon Coca-Cola sign with a time and temperature clock that had faced north on Peachtree Street for 30 years. It was on top of a Dunkin' Donuts shop that was taken down to build Margaret Mitchell Square. Many Atlantans protested the decision to remove the sign, and many more ultimately purchased pieces of the "retired" sign as cherished keepsakes. But the creation of Margaret Mitchell Square was much appreciated by the city's residents.

When G-P first announced its move to Atlanta, it cited "the contribution made by the arts to the quality of life" in the city as a chief factor in the decision. Three years after the building opened, G-P itself made a strong contribution to the arts scene in Atlanta by opening a downtown branch of the city's High Museum on the south side of the building. Upon the branch's opening in 1985, the *Atlanta Journal-Constitution* editorialized: "The Atlanta skyline has been enriched in more ways than one by the contributions of the new kid on the block." The three-story structure, with ramps and skylights, has hosted a wide variety of exhibits, including the extensive personal photographic collection of part-time Atlanta resident Elton John at the end of 2000.

homebuilding market in 1980, and the resulting slump seriously wounded G-P's building products business. Energy costs raged upward. Flowerree's initial run for glory hit a wall. Sales in 1980 were flat at $5 billion, while net income plunged from $327 million to $244 million, despite a 25 percent cutback in the capital-spending budget Flowerree had announced earlier in the year. The year before, in happier times, he had increased the capital-investment budget for his five-year plan from $2 billion to $2.75 billion.

Flowerree took the unusual step of writing an urgent letter to all 44,000 G-P employees to explain the depth of the crisis.

"Inflation, much like an unwanted guest, is literally eating America out of house and home," he wrote. "Mortgage interest rates have soared to unbelievable levels. The prime lending rate is approaching 20 percent. Quite plainly, the housing industry — our bread and butter — is weakening much faster than the experts predicted."

The next year was even worse. While G-P's sales edged up 8 percent to $5.4 billion in 1981, net income plummeted by a third to $160 million. The economic slump affected the paper business as well as building products. That year, G-P arranged two floating-rate revolving credit lines totaling $650 million.

The company's debt had risen to $1.66 billion, and the floating-rate portion made G-P particularly susceptible to the wild upswing of interest rates. The company was headed directly into what many observers believe was the most severe crisis in G-P's history.

The inflation had been great for Georgia-Pacific initially, as for any commodity business when prices begin rising. "We were kind of minting money for a while," recalls Danny Huff, a young accountant at the time who became executive vice president of finance and chief financial officer in 1999. Rather than buying back stock with excess cash, G-P poured the money into the pulp and paper and chemical businesses, he says.

But the minting of money didn't last. The recession drastically slowed homebuilding. At the same time, the runaway inflation sent G-P's floating interest rates skyrocketing. "We were spending money faster than we were making it," Huff says, "and we got in a situation where debt had crept up. Unfortunately, a lot of that debt was floating-rate, and interest rates were going through the roof. So we did have a crisis."

The crisis was three-fold. The sudden changes in the economy hit at precisely the time the company was moving its corporate headquarters from Portland to Atlanta. Just as G-P's income dropped and debt costs rose, the company was building an enormous new headquarters building, paying for 200 employees to make the move and underwriting their mortgages. Now the generosity of the company's earlier offer came back to haunt it: By the time of the move in 1982, the mortgage rates nationally were roughly twice the 8.5 percent the company had promised employees, and the company had to eat the difference. To make matters even worse, the company simply did not have the necessary safeguards in place to handle

such an unexpected disharmonic convergence of bad tidings.

"That was a scary time for those of us who knew about it," Huff says. "The fellow who was the cash manager at the time, Steve Coulter, was riding the elevator out in Portland with Jack McGovern, who was vice president of project financing. Steve mentioned to Jack: 'Do you realize we're out of cash?' McGovern immediately went up to CFO Harry Kane's office and asked him the same question. Kane couldn't believe it, but the fact was we were right up against the limit of our revolving credit."

Kane and McGovern immediately launched a plan to line up additional funds. Because the company was up against its limit at its traditional banks, it quickly set out to find new sources of loans. Borrowing domestically at that time proved to be very difficult, so G-P pulled off a Eurobond offering and put together a foreign bank syndicate to raise money that "really saved us at that point," Huff recalls. "That was a ticklish time for us."

Huff helped put together an emergency program to find out where the money was hemorrhaging. "We found we were spending money faster than we were making it by some margin. We were able then to cease some capital projects that were going on in chemicals and other places, or slow them back so that we could get through the crisis."

What McGovern and Huff experienced at that time ultimately led them to institute ultraconservative safeguards that would serve the company well in decades ahead and enable G-P to make large acquisitions that

Robert Flowerree, opposite, moved Georgia-Pacific to Atlanta but witnessed a dramatic slowdown in the economy after his spectacularly successful early years as chairman and CEO. By 1979, G-P's net income had reached $327 million on sales of $5.2 billion. In 1980, *Fortune* magazine said that for the first 25 years of the Fortune 500, G-P ranked second in sales growth, second in earnings per share growth and fourth in stock performance; $100 invested in G-P stock in 1954 was worth $6,056 in 1979. But by 1980, double-digit mortgage rates hammered the housing market — and Georgia-Pacific.

Building products slumped terribly during the early 1980s, but Georgia-Pacific continued to grow its paper business, expanding production and improving the product mix at the company mills in Florida and Arkansas. The rolls at right have been cut from huge parent rolls at the Crossett paper mill and will be cut further into packages of office paper. Today, this paper is sold to such customers as Staples, Sam's Clubs, Office Max and other large office-supply stores.

it otherwise might not have accomplished.

As soon as it became clear the company would weather the immediate crisis, G-P started issuing long-term fixed-rate debt under a plan devised by McGovern. "That really kind of enabled us both to carry more debt so we could get our cost of capital down and to minimize the refinancing risk," Huff says.

KANE ON THE HOOK

During the time of the floating-rate crisis, the attention of board members began to focus on one man: Harry Kane, who was having a personal investment crisis of his own.

Kane was widely admired, even beloved, by the people who worked for him. He was a gregarious, flamboyant man of Irish descent, a most unlikely CFO who looked more like a sales dandy — wearing the occasional pink sports jacket — than a dour numbers man. The mere mention of his name could bring tears to the eyes of his devotees 20 years later.

Kane hosted lavish golf outings for his staff, loading up a bus to travel out of Portland for a day of golf topped off with a big dinner. With 50 people in the room, Kane would walk up behind one person or another at each table and tell a personal story, touching or funny, about the person.

"He would tell it in a way that showed he had very personal knowledge of the person," Huff says. "That felt great. It was a real talent. He was full of stories and history about the old days that got people fired up. He'd do the same thing with the bankers."

Huff recalls a lavish meeting Kane set up with bankers in New York in 1981 to arrange loans for G-P. Kane invited 81 bankers. The gathering was more show than meeting. He gave a presentation about G-P's plans, and then passed out books that had a list of bank names with a dollar amount beside each name. "Each of the invited bankers had a little signature line at the bottom, and everybody was just expected to sign up," Huff says. "And they did. They all just loved it.

"Harry Kane was a tremendous individual. He was probably one of the most charismatic finance people I ever met in my life. I have a very warm spot in my heart for Harry, and I think he could get his whole organization to jump off a cliff for him. But my sense was that he didn't have the confidence of the board that all of us thought he should have. He was very good at accounting. He was a brilliant guy. But he didn't know much about corporate finance, and that's kind of why we got into such a serious problem with debt. He had the foresight to hire Jack McGovern because he knew he had a problem with corporate finance. I give him credit for solving the problem because he brought in the right resources to do it. I think he was a very effective CFO. It's just that he had bad circumstances."

Bob Flowerree also had kind words for Kane years later, but pointed out the flaw that ultimately caused unprecedented turmoil at the company's highest level. "Harry Kane did a great job until he started investing in stuff he shouldn't have been," Flowerree says, noting that company policy forbade officers from running

outside businesses that might distract them from their corporate responsibilities. "The idea was you worked for G-P 100 percent."

Kane invested heavily in real estate projects with his personal funds, Flowerree recalls. But a project in Hawaii was held up by legal challenges, and then the interest rates soared. "It distracted him very badly," Flowerree says.

The distractions could not have come at a worse time for Kane. Board members grew concerned that the company's CFO might have to declare personal bankruptcy, a legal action that could become a huge public embarrassment and perhaps degrade the market's confidence in Georgia-Pacific, exacerbating the company's financial problems.

According to Marion Talmadge, several board members told Floweree in January 1983 that he would have to ask Kane to resign if the CFO would not discontinue spending time on his personal ventures. But the board members did not stop with Kane.

Harvey "Bud" Fruehauf Jr., who was a member of that board, and several directors discussed the need for a change at the top outside of board meetings, sharing a growing concern that the company was so encumbered by floating-rate debt that it could not grow. "There was a progression of events," Fruehauf recalls. "I know that I had a lot of discussion with the other directors offline about where we were going and how we were going to have trouble getting where we wanted to go. We could see it was time for a management change. It wasn't done in a board meeting out in the open. Several of the directors and I talked about it

among ourselves and decided what had to be done. We discussed it with Bob Flowerree beforehand. We did it officially at a board meeting. There was some tension, of course, but no big problem. We wound up installing Marshall Hahn as chairman and a new slate of top officers."

Flowerree graciously agreed to step down, Fruehauf says, and remained in Atlanta for several more months to ensure a smooth transition. Harry Kane resigned as well. Flowerree moved back to Portland, after spending only one year in the city to which he had moved

Georgia-Pacific. Asked why he decided to return to Portland, he gestures toward the majestic view from his window with a smile and says, "Look around you." He remains low-key and philosophical about the end to his career as chairman. "It was just unfortunate, that's all," he says. "The market died."

Nearly 20 years later, Flowerree is still proud of his role in keeping G-P devoted to the basics of low-cost production. "I was an operations guy," he says. "I spent most of my time growing G-P and making the company the low-cost producer."

In 1983, Marshall Hahn replaced Robert Flowerree as chairman. Here, he presents a custom-made Purdy shotgun as a retirement gift to Flowerree, who moved back to Oregon. Flowerree said the reverses in the economy were unfortunate — "The market died." Hahn quickly went to work trying to save the company.

CHAPTER FIVE

Back from the Brink

Cover Your Ears. **Safety First!**

Marshall Hahn first came to Robert Pamplin's attention because of his success at the helm of the CEO's alma mater, Virginia Polytechnic Institute. But what caught Pamplin's eye wasn't necessarily the fact that Hahn tripled the enrollment and brought in millions of dollars for new buildings on the Blacksburg campus. What really gave rise to Pamplin's admiration was Hahn's reputation for toughness, which grew out of his hardnosed response to a protest by VPI students in 1970.

As recounted by *Fortune* magazine, students protesting the Vietnam War barricaded themselves inside a campus building. Rather than negotiate, "Hahn called in police, who ripped off the doors and hauled the protestors off to jail. When the students were released, Hahn kicked them out of school," *Fortune* wrote. The episode had a dampening effect on protest at Virginia Tech after that.

"Marshall told those crazy kids what the rules were and they wouldn't stop, so he got the law in and had them severely punished," Pamplin told *Fortune*. "I liked that."

Pamplin invited Hahn to join the G-P board of directors in 1973 and then hired him as an executive vice president in 1975, putting him in charge of the chemical division. Hahn described his role as "a high-priced trainee," but he was a high-priced trainee with

a burning desire to succeed. As he later described his childhood to *Fortune*, Hahn recalled eating Kentucky Wonder green beans from the family garden during the Depression: "When you're a kid and you eat a great big plate of green beans with no meat, well, a few hours later you feel like you're just starving. I said to myself — sort of like Scarlett O'Hara — 'I'm not going to be hungry again.'"

At the time Hahn joined G-P, Jim Kuse was running the chemicals business. Hahn was brought in over him and later acknowledged the grace with which Kuse handled the awkward situation. "We had a very strong person in charge of chemicals in Jim Kuse," Hahn recalls. "It could have been a sticky situation, but I came in with an attitude, 'Look, I need to learn from you fellows.' Jim did everything he could to help me learn and succeed."

T. Marshall Hahn Jr., Ph.D.,
left, was recruited by Robert
Pamplin because of the
toughness he exhibited as
president of Virginia Tech.
An admirer told *Fortune*
magazine that Hahn had steel
in his spine, worked like the
dickens and was "the smartest
man I've ever met." At first,
Hahn led the effort to save
Georgia-Pacific following the
financial problems of the
early 1980s, eliminating all
new spending that wasn't
needed for safety or the
environment. Later in his
tenure, he worked on
improving the company's
safety record, opposite.

Hahn was grateful to Flowerree as well. "Bob Flowerree was also one of my tutors," Hahn recalls. "He recognized that when I joined the company, I knew little or nothing about the business, and he was a patient teacher." Hahn rose quickly through the ranks. Within a year, he added the pulp and paper division to his chemical duties, then became president. In 1983, he was named CEO.

The transition between Flowerree and Hahn could have been acrimonious, but it went well because of Flowerree's gracious nature, Hahn recalls. "I was particularly impressed with his help in smoothing my transition to CEO. He was, as always, a gentleman and always helpful. And again, he displayed those characteristics of integrity, loyalty and commitment that are characteristic of Georgia-Pacific."

CRUNCH TIME

Davis Mortensen looks back on Hahn's early days as a crucial period when G-P could have gone either way. "Marshall took over from Bob Flowerree at a very difficult time, and I would say that Marshall and Stan Dennison did yeoman's work in saving the company," Mortensen says. "We were strapped for cash, business was not good and a lot of tough decisions had to be made."

John Rasor, who had worked his way up from an hourly position to become an officer of the company in 1983, arrived at the top only to find officers' salaries slashed by 10 percent. "I got there just in time for 'Here's your promotion — and your pay cut!' It was

a combination of both the downturn of the cycle and the financial state of the company at that time."

The financial crunch was so tight, Rasor recalls, "we hangared airplanes and sold one Citation on the broker's market for cash. Then we sold a plywood plant and a sawmill — if not two sawmills — out of the Crossett operations, and I remember making the call back to the dining room in Atlanta. Stan Dennison had given me the phone number and told me to call him whatever time it was to let him know, so he could be assured that the deal had closed. I think they were counting the cash that closely. The $2 million or $4 million sale of an asset was making a difference in terms of what the total cash position of the company was, and it was very close."

The tough times reverberated throughout the company. Rasor recalls that Larry Shorey, a "fireball" plywood plant manager in Mississippi, was told by his boss, Don Foster, that his salary increase was going to amount to only $15 per month. "Larry said, 'Don, if the company is in this bad a shape, just keep the $15 and let me do my work,'" Rasor says. "There was a very clear awareness on the part of every manager in Georgia-Pacific about what the state of affairs of the company was, at least financially."

At one point, rumors swept through the company that Georgia-Pacific itself was for sale, Rasor recalls.

"The cash flow problem was desperate when I assumed the CEO role," Marshall Hahn acknowledges. "We did everything we could to pull in our belt, so we basically stopped capital spending that didn't affect safety or environmental concerns. Not only did we have all that debt — roughly $2 billion — but the company was losing money and the market for our products was terrible and getting worse."

Even when the company began to get back on solid footing, the crisis loomed large in everyone's mind, Hahn says. "As we started to turn the finances around, we got just barely back in the black. To give you an idea of how tentative the recovery was, we were in the dining room one day and someone dropped some plates. As the plates shattered, one of the officers said, 'Uh, oh! We're in the red again!' We all had a good laugh, but those were tough days. We had a lot of 12- and 14-hour days."

Dennison, who served as Hahn's executive vice president, retained a brash, maverick spirit even years into retirement. As he looked back on the days when he and Hahn came together to plot their strategy, he concedes they were so confident they could pull off a turnaround that they were cocky about it: "It was fairly simple. We both agreed the company was saved."

"We worked our asses off, day and night in 1983," Dennison recalls. "We interviewed for a chief legal officer and a CFO up and down the East Coast. We gave each division a real hard lecture: 'You do your work; you do it well and do it in this manner. This is what's required of you.'"

Hahn also relied on Bob Schumacher, who had been running the Northeast division and was elevated to president. "Stan Dennison and Bob Schumacher and I spent an awful lot of time trying to figure out how we were going to get out of the mess that we were in," Hahn recalls. "There was a fair amount of

favorable publicity at one point when I borrowed some money and bought some of our stock at $20 a share. People asked, 'Well, why didn't you buy it when it was $13?' And I said, 'I wasn't sure we were going to make it then.' I laughed, and I remember folks laughing with me. That was just a joke. Those were some challenging days, all right. It took us a year or two of steady climbing to get to the point where there was a strong cash flow again, but we all knew the entire time that we were going to make it."

CORE FOCUS

When he took over, Hahn brought out the long knife and began divesting businesses in an attempt to get the company back in the black. He set out to keep what worked and stick close to Georgia-Pacific's roots.

"What Georgia-Pacific was doing well then was running its big mills," Hahn says. "We had gotten into a lot of other things. We were making paper labels, a little teeny operation, and paper plates and milk cartons. In all cases, these were small operations and we were not doing well with them. And we sold those operations as quickly as we could. The proceeds helped us with the debt problem and also allowed us to focus back on our businesses."

Under Hahn's debt reduction program, the company immediately withdrew from an Indonesian kraft paper project started by Bob Flowerree. G-P sold its furniture business and marginal plywood operations. Then Hahn took a good look at a civil antitrust case with a potential liability to the

Marshall Hahn began selling off non-strategic businesses to return Georgia-Pacific to its core focus and what it did best — running big mills. Among the businesses cut was the furniture business, above.

When he took over, Hahn brought out the long knife and began divesting businesses in an attempt to get the company back in the black. He set out to keep what worked and stick close to Georgia-Pacific's roots.

When Georgia-Pacific recovered sufficiently to begin expanding again, Marshall Hahn set out to buy some of the nation's best-run mills. The first was the showcase property of the St. Regis Corporation, a containerboard mill in Monticello, Mississippi, which G-P acquired in 1984. This cardboard box plant in Ashboro, North Carolina, is one of 15 that came along with the Monticello mill and timberland.

company of $2 billion.

"When I got the reins, we had a series of problems — we had very high debt when interest rates were spiking at 20 percent, we were losing money and we had hanging over our heads this plywood pricing case," Hahn recalls. "The company had been found innocent of the government charges, which would have been the criminal charges, but that was followed by a series of civil suits."

Some manufacturers had already settled out of the suit, but their share of the market was not carved out of the liability. Hahn personally went to Washington, with former Attorney General Griffin Bell, to lobby for the carve-out. "Senator Strom Thurmond was particularly helpful," Hahn says. In addition, the company successfully petitioned the U.S. Supreme Court for a writ of *certiorari* to review the case. With these "glimmers of hope," Hahn says, G-P proceeded to settle the case for approximately $99 million.

"We got rid of that $2 billion liability that was hanging over our heads. We couldn't do any financing with that big an unknown, and so that was one of the needed steps to get the company to a position where it could move again."

Hahn also recognized the value of G-P's strategic distribution network of huge warehouses spread throughout the country. He added even more centers.

As Georgia-Pacific returned to health in 1984, Hahn began expanding the pulp and paper operations. He said he wanted to increase pulp and paper to the same size and profitability as building products. "A better balance between these two sectors will allow us

to make more efficient use of our timber resources and also help further reduce our exposure to the residential construction cycle," he wrote in the annual report. G-P announced plans to install one of the world's largest white paper machines at Port Hudson, Louisiana, and upgraded equipment in mills at Palatka, Florida, and Crossett, Arkansas, to move further into higher margin grades of bleached paper and board.

But the biggest step would require the sort of creative financing that originally won the West for Owen Cheatham and Bob Pamplin.

Hahn and his team, which soon included James Van Meter as chief financial officer, not only scoured the G-P landscape for assets to sell, but also drew up a list of the best mills in America. Because Hahn had already decided that running big mills was what G-P did best, he wanted to make sure that G-P's mills *were* the best. The wish list of the best mills not then owned by G-P reached 10. In less than a decade, Hahn would acquire five of them.

The first was the showcase property of the St. Regis Corporation, a containerboard mill in Monticello, Mississippi, plus 275,000 acres of timberland to feed the mill. "Monticello was probably the most efficient containerboard mill in the country," Hahn recalls. Containerboard is the material used in making corrugated boxes. G-P's only other containerboard plant at the time was in Toledo, Oregon.

In early 1984, Hahn saw an opportunity arise in the wake of controversial corporate raiders and "greenmailers" in an era when deep-pocketed financiers bought sizeable portions of corporations, then

At left, an operator monitors presses at the Monticello mill, which Hahn called "probably the most efficient container-board mill in the country." Hahn's clever deal-making made industry competitors jealous, even prompting one to comment, "The St. Regis deal was a steal. They caught us flat-footed."

In 1984, Georgia-Pacific spun off its commodity chemical business to a management group led by James R. Kuse, pictured (right) with Director John D. Bryan in the Atlanta headquarters of Georgia Gulf Corporation. Though the business and its leadership began under a burden of significant debt, Georgia Gulf topped $1.5 billion in revenues in 2000, a gratifying success.

sold them back at a premium.

One of the most feared of these financiers was Sir James Goldsmith, who was viewed "as a bit of a rogue and a financial buccaneer by many in corporate America," according to an article in *Business Atlanta* magazine. Goldsmith raided two paper companies in the early 1980s, Crown Zellerbach and Diamond International. "His 1982 acquisition of Diamond gave him the reputation of an asset-stripper and bust-up artist," *Business Atlanta* wrote. One of Goldsmith's next targets was St. Regis.

The British financier bought an 8.6 percent stake in St. Regis for $109 million. The company bought it back for $160 million. The profit was so quick and delicious that another investor, Laurence A. Tisch, chairman of Loews Corporation, promptly moved in and bought an almost identical 8.5 percent stake in St. Regis.

Hahn saw Tisch's move as an opportunity for Georgia-Pacific.

"The shareholders of St. Regis obviously weren't enthusiastic about the fact that the management had paid a ransom to get out from under the Goldsmith threat, and so they were struggling with what to do," Hahn recalls. "I called St. Regis' chairman, Bill Haselton, and suggested that we would buy the stock from Tisch and then we would trade it back to them and we would have to work out relative values for Monticello and the timberlands that fed the mill. He thought that was a good idea."

Hahn and Van Meter met with Haselton and his CFO at a New York hotel, but the St. Regis boss wouldn't agree to anything with so many people in the room. So Hahn and Haselton met alone. "We agreed on what was a very attractive price from our perspective, and I wrote down the agreement in longhand, including an agreement that the day before the deal closed they would terminate all their employees and be responsible for all of the retirement benefits and then we would rehire those we were going to keep the next day, which saved us a big pot of money," Hahn recalls. "So we got that part of the deal done, and then the question was buying the stock."

Hahn returned to Atlanta, but Tisch said he would only deal with Hahn and had to see him immediately in New York, because he had only one night available.

"Our planes were scattered, so Van Meter and I chartered a jet and flew out of Atlanta at four in the afternoon and got to New York," Hahn says. "We started out in a big room at a hotel with our investment banker, Joe Perella, and our lawyers and Larry Tisch and his sons. We weren't getting very far because Tisch wanted to get at least as much for the stock per share as Goldsmith had gotten, and it wasn't appropriate to pay that.

"Larry Tisch didn't want to give any ground in front of his sons, so he suggested, 'Why don't I meet with this young man — meaning me — and see what we can work out.' So we worked on it until two or three in the morning, and we finally struck a deal where we agreed to pay the same amount per share as Goldsmith had gotten, but a good portion of that was going to be an interest-free note payable over several years, which, of course, reduced the value that we were paying. He and I shook hands, got everybody else back in the room and advised them of the terms, and Larry said, 'Okay, now, we got this worked out. You guys write up the agreement, and this young man and I are going to the restaurant for breakfast.'

"His son said, 'Well, Dad, the restaurant is closed.' But Tisch, who owned the Carlyle Hotel on Madison Avenue, said, 'That's okay. We'll go wake up the chef.' And we did. We had breakfast, came back and signed the deal. We ended up getting the mill and the timberlands for about half of what St. Regis insisted they would have to have."

According to the *New York Times*, the $374 million deal "gave Georgia-Pacific a long-sought plant in the South, eliminated Loews as a potentially dangerous stockholder in St. Regis and handed Loews an estimated $38.4 million pretax profit." As part of the deal, G-P became a friendly investor in St. Regis for five years. Along with the paper mill and timberlands came 15 cardboard box plants.

A year later, *Business Week* looked back on Hahn's Monticello deal and quoted an unnamed industry competitor as saying, "The St. Regis deal was a steal. They caught us flat-footed."

Not only did Hahn acquire Monticello, he also remade it. G-P managers extended the duration of the daily run at the mill, increasing its output from 1,500 to 1,800 tons of paper a day. Then G-P rebuilt the machines, and capacity increased to 2,700 tons a day.

"We added 1,200 tons a day — which in reality was a whole new mill," Hahn told *Fortune*. "That's sort of our style."

To help pay for Monticello, Hahn decided to sell the commodity chemicals business he had once headed. "We made the decision to sell that business, keeping only the specialty chemical business, where we could add value," Hahn says. "We attempted to sell the commodity chemical business on the outside. We could not do so at an attractive price, so we sold it for a combination of cash and debt and warrants to a management group led by Jim Kuse."

Kuse and four other executives bought 14 chemical plants in six states for $270 million and created Georgia Gulf Corporation in December 1984 through a leveraged buyout. The new company went public in 1986. Kuse remained chairman of Georgia Gulf until his death in 2001, just five months after the company topped $1.5 billion in revenues for the year 2000. Kuse and his team often talked about the enormous leap they made when leaving the G-P fold.

"They were all personally in debt as well as taking on huge debt in the company," Georgia Gulf general counsel Joel I. Beerman told the *Atlanta Journal-Constitution*. "Jim used to tell me he went to bed at night worrying, 'Are we going to be able to make payroll?' We always made payroll, but it was not a slam dunk."

Hahn recalls that not only did he package debt with the chemical business, "but we also took warrants, so as they got it to a higher multiple, the G-P shareholders would benefit more, too." When judging the legacy of Georgia-Pacific, it is important to remember that it spun off two large, successful enterprises — Georgia Gulf and Louisiana-Pacific — yet

Among the 14 chemical plants that formed Georgia Gulf was this plant in Plaquemine, Louisiana. The plant, pictured above in 1981, produces aromatics and chlorovinyls purchased by a variety of industries, including building products, paper products, medical and surgical supplies, agricultural and automotive products, paints and varnishes, pharmaceuticals and computer casings.

Georgia-Pacific's paper products business in the 1980s included office and printing papers, above and right, and consumer and commercial tissue products, opposite. G-P's "away-from home" tissue products — products used by hotels and restaurants and for janitorial supplies, provided a solid base for the expansion of G-P's tissue business with several major acquisitions in the 1990s.

°FELTWEAVE:
THE ELOQUENCE
OF A
WELL-CHOSEN
HAT

kept growing on its own while G-P stockholders benefited from the transactions.

Hahn's strategy caught the eye of *Business Week* in April 1985. "Hahn says he is using the same 'analytical approach, with an emphasis on the bottom line,' that he learned in engineering and mathematics as he redirects Georgia-Pacific," the magazine said. "He wants to transform a company that has mainly earned its way in plywood and other building supplies into a major papermaker."

Georgia-Pacific sold its Exchange Oil & Gas Corporation for $180 million in 1985. G-P had originally acquired the company to assure the natural gas supply for the methanol plant in Plaquemine, Louisiana. The company had some successes in exploration but believed the business could be more valuable to another company.

Later in 1985, the massive complex at Crossett, Arkansas, was hit by a strike. The labor union officials were not prepared for the toughness of the former

Virginia Tech president who had cracked down so hard on campus protestors a decade and a half earlier.

Hahn had experienced a seven-month strike by the Association of Western Pulp and Paper Workers at the Bellingham and Toledo plants when he was executive vice president of pulp, paper and chemicals. In the paper industry, companies had never attempted to operate a mill when the workers were on strike. Hahn had other ideas.

"I didn't know any better, so I said, 'Well, we can bring in workers from around the country and salaried people,'" he recalls. "And we operated those mills out there for seven months."

Secretaries and executive assistants moved from sedentary office jobs into the brash worlds of enormous mills. Some of the strikers were not at all pleased with Hahn. "One big old bruiser, he was a first hand on a paper machine, came to me one day and said, 'Now, my sister is a secretary, and she's in there running one of those paper machines. I understand what you are doing, and I respect it. But if she gets hurt, I'm coming after you,'" Hahn recalls. "In fact, we had better safety records with the salaried employees running the mills than we did with regular workers. We set production records with salaried personnel and also painted the mills and really lessened considerably the value of that sanction for the unions."

The Crossett strike by the United Paperworkers' International Union was one of the most acrimonious in G-P history. Hahn went a step farther than he had during the West Coast strikes, hiring replacement workers for the Crossett mill and putting it back in operation. "The Crossett strike in 1985 was particularly significant because it was the first strike in the paper industry in which permanent replacements were hired," wrote Timothy J. Minchin, a history professor, in an article in the *Arkansas Historical Quarterly* in 2000.

The Crossett strike lasted three months, ended in union defeat and bitterly divided the mill community, Minchin wrote, because local residents took the jobs of their neighbors and union members left the picket lines to return to work. Hahn acknowledges there was

Employees make quality checks on a Coronet towel production line in Palatka, Florida, in the 1980s. They are wearing t-shirts expressing Palatka's local quality slogan — "If I wouldn't buy it … I won't pack it!" Georgia-Pacific facilities traditionally have had a great deal of autonomy.

Despite his reputation for toughness, Hahn also had a wry sense of humor. One year when he couldn't attend a Christmas party, he posed for a picture that was made into a life-sized cutout, complete with Santa hat, right. In 1986, Hahn moved Georgia-Pacific into the premium bath tissue market with the introduction of Angel Soft, opposite. The company's ad campaign, featuring winged babies, drew raves from the advertising press. In 1988, *Business Week* noted that in just 18 months, Angel Soft captured 6 percent of the $2 billion tissue market against marketing giants Scott Paper Company and Procter & Gamble.

some lingering resentment after the strike but that labor and management ultimately got back on good terms. "That has always been a very good labor force," he says.

HAHN AT THE HELM

Hahn made the transition from cost-cutting company savior to a business leader ready to take on new challenges. He was credited by virtually everyone who worked with him as a genius with a photographic memory. "He was one of the smartest men on the face of the earth," Dennison says. "He was calm, sincere, he listened and he acted when he had reached a decision that those involved thought was right. Then he left it to the operating officer to put it into effect."

Hahn also was known for his sharp sense of humor. "He can be a devil," recalls Don Blank, senior director for television, photography and technology communications. "In the annual budget review, before you'd even get started, he would find the most obscure item he figured you probably didn't have an

answer to. He'd say, 'Don, I'm really curious here as to why your meal budget went from $1,200 last year to $1,800 this year. Can you tell me a little bit about that?' He just loved to do that. He smiled, and you could see he was enjoying it."

One year, Hahn couldn't attend a Christmas party in the studio for all of the company's TV clients. Blank sent the company's photographer to take a picture of the chairman, which was converted into a life-sized cutout. "I put a Christmas hat on it and put it up in the studio and people came in and posed with the obvious cutout of the chairman. Hahn thought it was great." After that, the cutout became a moveable prank. People would hide it in darkened rooms and when someone would turn on the lights, they would suddenly be face-to-face with a life-sized facsimile of the CEO.

By 1986, under Hahn's leadership, the company was back on track. Sales exceeded $7 billion and net income was up 58 percent to $296 million from the year earlier. In a move that would later seem prescient, Georgia-Pacific introduced a higher-quality tissue, Angel Soft.

"That was the brainstorm of the Northeast division under the leadership of Mike Wilson," Hahn recalls. Wilson had to face Hahn in the standards review, asking for $10 million for an advertising campaign to support the new super-soft product.

"That was still in the times when we were very tight-fisted with our spending, so we agreed I would sleep on it because we had a two-day standards review," Hahn recalls. The extra time also gave Hahn time to devise a way to have a little fun with Wilson. The next day, he told Wilson he had had a nightmare the previous evening in which "this charming lady shareholder called me and said you named that product the wrong thing. You should have named it 'Rambo.' I said why do you want to call it Rambo? She said, 'Well, I tried your product, and it's rough and it's tough and it won't take nothing off nobody.' Actually, I didn't use exactly those words," Hahn says. "They called Mike Wilson 'Rambo' after that.

"We did decide to back that advertising program, and that was really the beginning of our pushing into the at-home tissue market as successfully as we did," Hahn says. The decision was applauded by *Business Week* in 1988, when it noted that G-P's Angel Soft TV spots featuring winged babies "have drawn raves from the ad press. In just 18 months, Angel Soft has captured an impressive 6 percent of the $2 billion tissue market against such heavyweights as Scott Paper Co. and Procter & Gamble."

As for Hahn's move into paper, *Business Week* recalled his earlier vow that G-P "would begin to cushion itself from the ups and downs of the housing market by pushing more heavily into pulp and paper products. Investors thought the silver-haired physicist and former college president ought to go back to his ivory tower. After all, pulp and paper were on the skids…. Since then, the paper market has recovered,

and a new Georgia-Pacific is making the most of it."

In addition to introducing Angel Soft in 1986, the company returned to acquisition mode full force, purchasing five hardboard plants, three molding plants and a kiln-dried hardwood lumber facility.

The 1986 annual report included a company timeline noting the astounding fact that an original investment of 1,000 shares of Georgia-Pacific stock at $8.20 per share in 1949, with splits and dividends, would have grown to the sum of $4,029,192 by December 31, 1986.

In 1987, Georgia-Pacific bought one of its oldest and toughest competitors, U.S. Plywood, for $208 million in cash. The transaction included distribution and shipping facilities, five sawmills, a plywood plant and 200,000 acres of timberland. G-P also bought the assets of Erving Distributor Products Co., including two tissue plants.

The rebound of G-P was moving along nicely, just in time for the stock market crash in October 1987. On "Black Monday," Danny Huff, then director of corporate finance, was attending the American Bankers Association Convention in Dallas when a financial official from Chrysler was summoned away from their table at lunch.

"He came back in with a look on his face and said, 'Guys, it's all over. The stock market crashed,'" Huff says. "Our stock price had been in the 50s and went down to 23 that day before it closed at 27."

That crash did not have long-lasting effects, although virtually every major American company's stock fell, Huff says. In retrospect, "it was a tremendous

opportunity to buy." But G-P didn't take the plunge in late 1987 because it was not ready to take on more debt, having just emerged from the company's darkest period.

CORRELL COMES ABOARD

A few months later, in early 1988, Hahn received a telephone call that led to the most important hire of his Georgia-Pacific career. It came out of the blue from a young paper executive at the Mead Corporation, A. D. "Pete" Correll.

"I got to know Pete when we were both representing our companies in labor negotiations on the West Coast. He was with Weyerhaeuser at the time, and I was with Georgia-Pacific," Hahn says. "I thought he was one of the most capable young men in the industry. One day, years later, when Pete was at Mead, he called me and said it looked like he had lost out in the race at Mead and asked if we had any jobs available.

"I said, 'Pete, I don't know what the job is or what it will pay, but for you, yeah, there's a job.' He said, 'All right, I'll take it.' That is the sort of mutual confidence we have in each other."

Correll joined the company as senior vice president of pulp and printing paper, reporting to Conrad Schweitzer, whom he would later succeed as executive vice president of pulp and paper. The transition from a position in which he was competing for the chief executive job at one company to a senior vice presidential job at another was difficult. Many G-P

An original investment of $1,000 in Georgia-Pacific stock in 1949 would have grown, with splits and dividends, to more than $4 million by the end of 1986. In 1987, Georgia-Pacific weathered the stock market crash and bought one of its oldest and most bitter competitors, U.S. Plywood, for $208 million, including distribution and shipping facilities, five sawmills, a plywood plant and 200,000 acres of timberland. Plywood, opposite and above, remained a staple of G-P's building products business.

The acquisition of Brunswick Pulp & Paper Company for $667 million gave G-P three sawmills and 535,000 acres of timberlands and included the pulp and paperboard mill above and the wood yard opposite. The Brunswick facility was a joint venture of Scott Paper Company and the Mead Corporation. Former Mead executive Pete Correll had just joined G-P and helped lead the integration of the new facility.

talked to me. It was horrible. Georgia-Pacific simply did not like outsiders. And they certainly didn't like outsiders coming in at my level."

Correll says the only person who would speak to him was a G-P executive named Clint Kennedy, who quickly became his best friend. "Clint said he knew from the moment we talked that I was going to be the one running pulp and paper someday. We got along great. We never had any issues. He was a good guy. He had very strong sales and marketing skills and wanted to learn some general management and manufacturing skills. I learned a lot from him in one area, and he learned a lot from me in the other."

Correll's isolation didn't last long. He joined the company in February, and in August, Hahn purchased the giant Brunswick Pulp & Paper Company, for $667 million in Brunswick, Georgia, Correll's home-town. It was a mill he had supervised at Mead.

"It was a big deal. We bought the mill, 535,000 acres of timberland and three sawmills from Scott Paper and Mead," Correll says. "I think that kind of thrust me into the in-crowd. I brought that whole organization in, and they all used to work for me at Mead. That was what broke the ice for me. After that, I was part of the team."

The Brunswick mill was one of the "Top 10" that Hahn had identified earlier. It was a joint venture between Mead and Scott Paper Company. The mill produced around 1,500 tons a day of bleached softwood market pulp and 500 tons a day of bleached paperboard, used to make products such as folding cartons, paper plates and cups. The timber supply was

veterans did not warmly welcome the paper man from Mead.

"Joining Georgia-Pacific was kind of like moving to Russia and joining the Soviet Army," Correll says. "When I came in here, I was about the most unwelcome human who ever walked. Marshall gave me the title of senior vice president of pulp and printing papers, which meant I had our white paper business, all our pulp sales and all of our container-board sales. And when I showed up, I said, 'Where's my office?' They said, 'We don't have one for you. Go down there on the 12th floor and find one.' So they found me a little office, and I sat there. Nobody

strategically located to support the fiber needs of the Brunswick mill as well as G-P facilities in South Carolina, Georgia and Florida.

The massive Brunswick mill produced more chips than it could use, left, so they were shipped to other plants on the Eastern Seaboard. Chips could be loaded into the cargo holds of leased ships such as the *Julia*, above. Georgia-Pacific owned only one ship, the *Georgia S*, which was used to transport gypsum.

GREAT NORTHERN ACQUISITION

In the mid-1980s, as Georgia-Pacific returned to health, Hahn contacted then Bob Hellendale, president of Great Northern Nekoosa Corporation. "I had approached him in an effort to make a friendly acquisition or merger. He and I had some friendly discussions built on the foundation that if the discussions didn't go anywhere, we would not make an unsolicited offer for GNN as long as he was CEO, which we lived up to. But of course when he retired, the game was different."

The game began in late 1989 as the first major

#64 Paper Machine
The Ashdown Express
1991

unfriendly takeover in the forest products industry. Great Northern Nekoosa, a paper and pulp giant based in Norwalk, Connecticut, had 1989 revenues of $3.86 billion, roughly a third the size of G-P, which had 1989 revenues of $10.17 billion.

Driving the GNN acquisition was Hahn's philosophy of buying, rather than building, primary mills. Building a large mill adds capacity to the sometimes-glutted market. Buying one does not add capacity, but adds market share.

"That was a difficult acquisition," Hahn recalls. "After efforts to negotiate for the acquisition of that company were unsuccessful, we proceeded with an

unsolicited tender offer. That carried risks, both the risk of failing and the assumption of a high level of debt."

On October 31, 1989, G-P announced a $58-per-share tender offer for GNN. Hahn sent a letter to the new GNN chairman and CEO, William R. Laidig, requesting a meeting. He had called Laidig earlier in the week to alert him that an offer was coming. *Business Atlanta* magazine described the call as "perhaps the nastiest Halloween surprise" Laidig had ever received. G-P also announced that Bank of America would provide $1.25 billion of the financing and arrange a syndicate of banks for the remainder of the $3.1 billion bid.

"The offer was a stunning development in the forest-products business, which has long been dominated by a dozen major companies that generally dealt with one another on a friendly, almost gentlemanly basis," wrote the *New York Times*. Laidig said the G-P offer was uninvited and that GNN's board would consider the bid in due course.

GNN was incorporated in Maine, which had a "rigorous anti-takeover statute," the *Times* wrote. The newspaper also noted that some analysts questioned whether the G-P bid was a reasonable price. Gary Palmero, an analyst at Oppenheimer & Company, thought GNN was worth $78 per share — $20 more than G-P was offering. "Georgia-Pacific has a reputation of throwing around nickels like manhole covers," Palmero told the *Times*. "They are trying to get the company on the cheap."

The takeover turned into a monumentally ugly

public relations battle, with Laidig calling the offer from Georgia-Pacific "ill-conceived…surprising and disturbing." In turn, Hahn blasted GNN for approving rich golden parachutes for its executives. *Business Atlanta* characterized the takeover as "a noisy and bruising battle that included charges and counter-charges of lying, board irresponsibility, willful neglect, mismanagement, attempted union busting and gross misconduct. It sucked into its daily drama — played out largely in the press — the Federal Trade Commission, several state courts, influential institutional investors, a large contingent of superstar Wall Street advisers, the AFL-CIO, environmental groups, 19 banks representing an international Who's Who of lenders, and Maine's governor, attorney general and the entire state House."

The magazine described Hahn as "the strong-willed and charismatic executive who broke a taboo in the industry." Hahn started out the process by referring to Laidig as "my good friend." Laidig, described as a capable executive and a gentleman, took offense. "At one point in the game, Hahn kept referring to me as his friend, and I said, 'Well, we were business acquaintances, but not friends in the sense we hung out in the dance halls together,'" Laidig says.

When Hahn left the G-P building in Atlanta to do battle in court with Great Northern, Georgia-Pacific staffers cheered,

according to *Fortune* magazine. An admirer described him to the magazine: "He's got steel in his spine. He works like the dickens. And besides that, he's the smartest man I've ever met."

The state government of Maine was particularly on edge about the possible takeover because it had seen Sir James Goldsmith sell off vast tracts of Diamond International to land speculators and had recently experienced a bitter 16-month strike against International Paper Company in Jay, Maine.

The Maine connection brought Correll to the stage. He had earned two graduate degrees at the

Georgia-Pacific launched the industry's first hostile takeover in 1989, acquiring Great Northern Nekoosa Corporation for $5.4 billion. GNN had the world's largest, fastest paper machine — the Ashdown Express at Ashdown, Arkansas, opposite. The highly public battle cemented G-P's reputation for frugality. The company was said to be "throwing around nickels like manhole covers," and Hahn was presented with one as a gag, below.

University of Maine and was sent to testify in various forums in his old stomping grounds. "It was the damnedest thing you ever heard of in your life," Correll recalls. "I spent an ungodly amount of time on the witness stand in courtrooms or the legislature. In fact, there's actually a resolution passed by the Maine legislature that urges me to keep my word about how we would handle the properties we acquired."

The fight grew increasingly acrimonious until February 1990, when Laidig finally capitulated, saying, "The time has come for Great Northern Nekoosa to join Georgia-Pacific." GNN's shareholders agreed in March to go with the G-P offer. Georgia-Pacific paid

$65.75 per share, a total of almost $4 billion. When the battle ended, G-P had spent $200 million on legal and other fees resulting from lawsuits in state and federal courts in Maine and Connecticut, according to the *Atlanta Journal-Constitution*. The total payment would later rise to $5.4 billion after paying off GNN's debt. The purchase price exceeded the fair value of GNN's net assets by $2 billion, the G-P 1990 annual report stated, adding the $2 billion was included in goodwill and was being amortized over 40 years.

Within two months, G-P announced it was selling off $1 billion worth of assets to cut costs, raise capital and reduce debts incurred in the GNN takeover.

Among the jewels that Georgia-Pacific gained with the acquisition of Great Northern Nekoosa were the enormous complex at Ashdown, Arkansas, opposite, and the Leaf River pulp mill in New Augusta, Mississippi, above.

Georgia-Pacific inherited a major liability with the acquisition of the Leaf River plant — litigation filed by thousands of plaintiffs over the issue of dioxin discharges. Georgia-Pacific faced ruin, but its lawyers were triumphant — going 6-0 in the Mississippi Supreme Court and 9,140-0 at the trial courts. The company did not pay to settle any cases. G-P showed that the mill was not a source of dioxins in Southern Mississippi.

One of the problems with a hostile takeover is that the buyer can't perform due diligence to discover problems lurking beneath the surface of the target company. When Georgia-Pacific acquired Great Northern Nekoosa in 1990 it inherited a major liability — litigation filed by approximately 1,000 plaintiffs against the Leaf River pulp mill in New Augusta, Mississippi, over the issue of dioxin discharges.

Georgia-Pacific knew suits had been filed against the mill but didn't think there was a big problem. The dioxin emissions from the mill were infinitesimally small, and the company had taken action as soon as it learned of the emissions.

But the number of plaintiffs eventually swelled to 9,150 in 215 cases, and Georgia-Pacific found itself doing battle in Mississippi courtrooms with a cast of characters out of a Faulkner novel, including a juror who was also a plaintiff. The company came to realize that its entire fate was on the line. G-P's attorneys scrambled into action with one of the most original scientific cases in the history of toxic litigation and, in the eyes of Pete Correll, saved the company — and perhaps the industry.

"At first, it just wasn't viewed as a big deal," recalls Kenneth Khoury, Georgia-Pacific vice president and deputy general counsel who joined the company as an attorney in 1990. G-P had hired an impressive legal team, including Lee Davis Thames, one of Mississippi's top trial lawyers, to protect its interests against an aggressive Mississippi plaintiff's attorney named John Deakle.

In *American Lawyer*, a Louisiana lawyer described

Deakle by saying, "He can talk to a jury better than Jimmy Swaggart can talk to a congregation. He'll get them crying in the jury box." The prediction was on the mark.

The first trial was held in the Greene County courthouse, which featured a room one floor above the courtroom that had previously been used for indoor hangings.

The first plaintiff was Wesley Simmons, a retired commercial fisherman who lived next to the river 42 miles downstream from the mill. He claimed the mill's pollution had diminished the value of his property and caused him emotional harm because he feared contracting disease from eating contaminated fish.

"I just want to say that God created that river for everyone," Simmons testified, weeping. "He didn't create it for a few money-hungry people to destroy for every creature and every human and everything he put it there for. And I'm sorry I'm breaking down. I didn't want to, and I can't help it."

Thames presented testimony from G-P officials that once the company discovered dioxin was being emitted, it spent $8 million to reduce the emissions to nondetectable levels.

But the jury in the tiny town of Leakesville, Mississippi, was all Deakle's, even though he produced no evidence that Simmons had been exposed to dioxin. The jury returned a verdict in favor of Simmons for $40,700 in compensatory damages and $1 million in punitive damages.

Khoury recalls that it slowly began to dawn on company officials back in Atlanta that, "Oh, God. This could be serious."

Publicity from the verdict prompted a flood of new cases. Deakle's next case to go to trial was in Pascagoula, Mississippi, on behalf of Thomas and Bonnie Ferguson, a couple who lived 125 miles downstream from the mill on the Pascagoula River and claimed that between them they routinely ate 100 pounds of catfish a year from the river. They were joined in the suit by Louise Mitchell, who owned 1,000 acres of land on the Pascagoula.

To defend the second case, in January 1992, the G-P legal team brought in Gene Partain, a polished Atlanta lawyer who had won two dioxin cases for Hercules in Arkansas.

In the Ferguson case, Deakle delivered what *American Lawyer* called the "coup de grace to Georgia-Pacific" when he brought a retired navy admiral, Elmo Zumwalt Jr., to the stand as a rebuttal expert. Zumwalt had ordered the use of Agent Orange, a chemical defoliant containing dioxin, in Vietnam, but by the 1990s was an outspoken critic not only of dioxin but also of vague government and industry conspiracies.

Zumwalt's son had died of Hodgkin's disease ostensibly contracted as a result of exposure to Agent Orange in Vietnam as a navy lieutenant. Zumwalt also testified he believed dioxin led to birth defects in his two grandchildren. At least one juror wept during his testimony.

Although the plaintiffs had refused to have themselves tested for dioxin exposure, the Jackson County jury awarded the Fergusons $10,000 each for their nuisance claims and $90,000 each for their emotional distress and fear claims. Ms. Mitchell received no compensatory damages. Then the jury awarded the plaintiffs $3 million in punitive damages.

Suddenly, Georgia-Pacific was in big trouble. "The Ferguson verdict sent shock waves through Georgia-Pacific," says Khoury. "Things got really scary. The plaintiffs felt they had us on the run." Lawsuits were flying. G-P's competitors were settling similar dioxin suits — including International Paper, Temple-Inland, Weyerhaeuser, Kimberly-Clark, Procter & Gamble and Champion.

Marshall Hahn was chairman of G-P at the time and decided to fight back. Hahn and Pete Correll asked Ken Khoury, a mergers, acquisitions and finance lawyer by training, to take over the litigation.

Khoury hired a search firm to track down a defense lawyer who knew dioxin and hired Edward Fitzpatrick III from Dow Chemical. He also brought in high-priced talent such as David Boies of New York's Cravath, Swaine & Moore, who later represented Vice President Al Gore during the court fight over the Florida vote count in the 2000 presidential election, and a group of local Mississippi lawyers, like Joe Sam Owen of Gulfport, who could fight Deakle with the same tactics being used on G-P.

"From the first day, Marshall said, 'I don't care what it takes. I don't care what it costs. If we didn't do anything wrong, I just want to win,'" says Fitzpatrick.

Fitzpatrick later found out that after the Ferguson verdict, plaintiffs' lawyers in Mississippi got together and decided how they would "divide up" Georgia-Pacific's assets. "By the winter of 1992, Georgia-Pacific was road kill on the back roads of Mississippi," Fitzpatrick says.

The third case went to trial in 1993 with a different plaintiff's attorney, former judge Robert Pritchard of Pascagoula, who had opened a "dioxin office" to handle thousands of potential plaintiffs. He was representing two families, the Beeches and the Williams, who lived 67 miles below the mill. The families refused to test themselves or their properties for dioxins but claimed they suffered emotional distress and feared getting cancer from the fish they ate from the Pascagoula River.

Khoury won an important early victory when he had Zumwalt excluded from the trial because he was not qualified to testify as an expert. The judge read Khoury's brief and excluded Zumwalt without hearing any arguments. Pritchard was stunned.

Fitzpatrick brought in the world's top dioxin expert, Professor Christoffer Rappe from Sweden, who testified for G-P that the dioxins found on the Beeches' and Williamses' properties could not have come from a pulp mill.

The jury returned a verdict in favor of Georgia-Pacific, and the tide had turned, although the company still faced suits from more than 9,000 plaintiffs.

In 1994, Fitzpatrick worked with Rappe and began the most comprehensive study of dioxin in any area of the world. The team gathered a market basket of groceries in the Mississippi counties where most of the plaintiffs lived. Rappe's tests showed that all the items contained various types of dioxins. Incredibly, the tests showed that catfish grown on farms contained more dioxin than catfish from the Leaf River. Later, scientists determined that the dioxin came from the soybean meal fed to the catfish.

Georgia-Pacific was able to show — using scientific fingerprinting techniques — that the Leaf River mill was not the source of any dioxins or furans found in the Leaf or the Pascagoula Rivers or in any soil collected from the flood plains of the rivers.

After Georgia-Pacific's studies were presented at conferences, peer-reviewed and published, the company began filing summary judgment motions in the more than 200 pending cases. Georgia-Pacific argued that none of the plaintiffs presented proof of exposure to any substance from the Leaf River mill. In addition, Georgia-Pacific presented the results of its dioxin study as evidence that the mill was not a source of dioxins or furans in Southern Mississippi and that there were many other sources of dioxins and furans in the area.

Summary judgment was granted in all the remaining cases.

As Georgia-Pacific prepared for appeals of the first two cases, it discovered that one of the jurors in the Simmons case had signed a contract with Deakle to be a plaintiff against G-P in the future and, furthermore, had an agreement to share in any punitive damage awards. In other words, she voted in favor of a $1 million punitive award to Simmons in which she had a financial interest.

G-P eventually won both the Simmons and Ferguson cases on appeal in the Mississippi Supreme Court, as well as several plaintiff appeals.

"After being on the brink of disaster, Georgia-Pacific went 6-0 at the Mississippi Supreme Court, 9,140-0 at the trial courts and did not pay to settle any cases," Fitzpatrick says.

During G-P's dioxin studies, Fitzpatrick impishly sent a representative to a Mexican restaurant in Southern Mississippi that was owned by John Deakle and shipped a sample of the food to Sweden for testing. The results showed the food contained small amounts of dioxin, like most other samples they tested.

"We never used the Deakle restaurant results in court, but Marshall Hahn thought that out of all the funny, crazy things that we did, that was the most hilarious," Fitzpatrick says.

In 1991, the Northern spotted owl, opposite, came under the Endangered Species Act. The government banned logging in stands of old growth timber across more than seven million acres of federal land in the Northwest, closing an estimated 135 mills from several companies and putting loggers out of work. Ironically, the ban drove up the prices of timber and generated cash that the industry put back into paper.

A federal lawsuit claimed G-P had already had a specific plan to sell assets prior to the acquisition, which the company denied. "Obviously, we couldn't know what assets we wanted to sell until we had all the portfolio assets before us and knew what they were," Hahn says. "We couldn't do due diligence."

Correll was grilled heavily at one point because he had written a note in a G-P executive session that came to light in court. Correll wrote, "Keep the jewels and sell the dawgs." As a University of Georgia alumnus, Correll had used that school's favored spelling of "dogs." Hahn recalls the episode with delight: "Pete said on the stand that you have to understand that in Georgia, 'dawg' is a term of endearment."

Looking back, CFO Danny Huff says, "Clearly the GNN acquisition was the right thing to do. The problem is, we paid too much. The company was caught at the end of the leveraged buyout era and the companies' investment bankers and lawyers went to war. It was just an unfortunate series of events. You wanted to get the thing over with, and the only way to do that is to raise the price. You end up bidding against yourself."

"That was a real education for me," Correll says. "I told our board the tuition was very high, but I learned a hell of a lot. I had never been involved in a hostile takeover. I had never bought anything that you couldn't do adequate due diligence on, where you didn't know what you had until you had it. Because everything we dealt with, of course, was public information."

"It was a great strategic acquisition," Correll says. "But we paid too much for it, and the timing was wrong. We didn't know we paid too much until we knew the timing was wrong. Right after the acquisition, we went into a major downturn cycle in the pulp and paper business, which nobody had forecast at the time we did the deal. Reagan kept tightening down the economy, and suddenly we couldn't export anything. Prices crashed in the United States. It's very easy in retrospect to be critical of paying too much, but that wasn't what anybody in our industry thought would happen."

With the acquisition of Great Northern Nekoosa in 1990, G-P added 55 paper mills and paperboard converting plants, 83 paper distribution centers, one plywood plant and two sawmills. Sales for 1990 reached $12.7 billion. Most important, Hahn had added three more mills from his Top 10 wish list: Ashdown, Arkansas; Leaf River, Mississippi; and Cedar Springs, Georgia. In addition, Georgia-Pacific had become the number one papermaker in addition to being the world's largest distributor of building products.

Hahn's concerns about high debt proved to be well placed. "At the end of 1990," he says, "the debt level reached $7.6 billion. That was a debt to total capital ratio of over 63 percent. But, by the end of 1992, that debt was down to $6.1 billion."

NEW LEADERSHIP

In an article on the Great Northern acquisition, *Fortune* noted Correll's impact on the company, describing him as a respected strategist who was setting a new tone for G-P.

Georgia-Pacific continued
to pioneer new methods of
reforestation by producing
genetically improved
seedlings like this Southern
pine, right.

During the 1988 planting season alone, Georgia-Pacific reforested 100,000 acres of harvested land nationwide by planting 34.7 million fast-growing, disease-resistant seedlings or by natural reforestation.

In this enormous nursery in Cottage Grove, Oregon, left, Georgia-Pacific grows Douglas fir "super seedlings" that are genetically improved to fight disease and grow rapidly. G-P plants the seedlings in its own forests and also sells them to other companies. The young women below work with young seedlings that will take 14 to 16 months to reach a size suitable for planting.

In 1993, Georgia-Pacific entered a landmark agreement with the U.S. Fish and Wildlife Service to conserve the habitat of the endangered red-cockaded woodpecker on timberlands owned and managed by the company. On the picture above, Pete Correll wrote a note to G-P's Lee Thomas, former administrator of the Environmental Protection Agency: "To Lee Thomas, we couldn't have done this without you."

"We're becoming more rigorous in our analysis," Correll told the magazine, pointing out that G-P had used a full set of modern analytical tools in sizing up GNN. *Fortune* noted that McKinsey consultants were roaming corporate headquarters analyzing the tissue business. "We are taking the whole business apart," Correll said. "We've really changed." By this time, Correll had been promoted to executive vice president of pulp and paper. Ron Hogan had been promoted to president and chief operating officer, succeeding Harold L. Airington, who moved into the position of vice chairman.

In 1991, the logging practices in the Pacific Northwest returned to the front pages of the nation when the Northern spotted owl was included in a list of protected animals under the Endangered Species Act. To protect the habitat of this owl, the government instituted a ban against logging in stands of old growth timber older than 80 years across more than seven million acres of federal land in northern California, Oregon and Washington. As a result, an estimated 135 mills were closed, and unemployment reached 25 percent in some logging communities.

Ironically, the ban drove the prices of timber sky high. "The spotted owl gave us a big shot in the arm," says Danny Huff. "It was a supply issue. The spotted owl took all that government timber off the market, and the shortage raised the end product prices. That event saved a lot of people in this industry and generated a lot of cash that people put back into paper."

In the summer of the spotted owl, G-P's board announced that Hahn would stay on two years past

his 65th birthday. That would allow time for him to complete the training of his heir apparent. Pete Correll was elected president and chief operating officer and his chief competitor for the CEO's position, Ron Hogan, was promoted to vice chairman. He would leave G-P the next year.

Marshall Hahn says he always considered Correll a candidate to succeed him. "When I hired Pete, it was a very deliberate act of bringing in a CEO successor and then getting him ready. And I really felt he was ready when I was 65. We were still digesting the GNN acquisition, however, and the board asked me to stay on until I was 67, which I did. But I said at that time, 'Oh, I think he's ready.' I guess he was readier two years later."

Correll says his rise to the top took him by surprise. "I made a commitment to myself when I came to Georgia-Pacific that I was not going to enter corporate politics again, that I was not going to run a company, that I was going to work until I was about 60 years old and then hang it up. I had been in a race for the top position at the Mead Corporation. I entered a period when I didn't agree on where they were going and left. It was a very frustrating time in my life. So I came to Georgia-Pacific perfectly prepared to be a group vice president and run a major part of the company, work 45 hours a week and do my job. And suddenly I find myself right back in the middle of a race that I really did not intend to be in. But like a lot of old racehorses, once I got in it, I felt like I was, at that point in time, the most qualified person to run this company. Marshall worked two

more years to let me have that opportunity, and I owe him a lot for that."

During those years, Correll began to establish a name as an environmental leader, reaching a landmark agreement with Secretary of the Interior Bruce Babbitt to protect the endangered red-cockaded woodpecker on four million acres of G-P timberland in Arkansas, Louisiana, Mississippi and South Carolina. The company agreed to keep buffer zones around trees where the birds reside.

Correll was elected chairman in 1993, and Hahn moved into retirement, keeping the title of honorary chairman. Georgia-Pacific recorded $12.3 billion in sales for 1993, almost twice the $6.5 billion in net sales the company recorded in its first year under Hahn.

The former Virginia Tech president with a Ph.D.

from MIT had not only saved Georgia-Pacific, he had doubled its size. Looking back, Hahn says, "First, we refocused the company on its basic business. As a dimension of that, we recognized that we knew how to run big mills well. Second, because the big mills were the key to competitive success, we launched an effort to really become significant in the pulp and paper side. In the history of G-P, what little pulp and paper we had acquired had been pretty much a side effort to growing building products and the timber base.

"We moved from a company where pulp and paper was not the major dog in the team to where it was an equal partner with building products and acquired substantial timberlands in the process, too," Hahn says.

His protégé would take the company even further in that direction.

PETE CORRELL'S SEVEN POINTS OF LIGHT

Pete Correll, above, established himself as a charismatic leader in Georgia-Pacific when he delivered a dramatic speech in early 1989. Correll, who was succeeding Conrad Schweitzer as executive vice president of pulp and paper, ended his 47-page speech by saying "Well, folks, that's me, and that is what I believe." He was met by thunderous applause.

Only rarely can a corporate leader turn a company around with a single speech. But Pete Correll inspired a generation of Georgia-Pacific managers with the speech he delivered in West Palm Beach, Florida, on February 16, 1989, after he was named executive vice president of the pulp and paper division, succeeding the legendary Conrad Schweitzer.

Although he had been with G-P little more than a year, Correll had realized that the company's costs in pulp and paper were out of line with reality. "When this company decided to get into the pulp and paper business, it drifted away from its lean and mean philosophy," Correll says. Schweitzer had arranged to hold a meeting of the pulp and paper leaders, as well as leaders from the building products division, to celebrate a record year in 1988.

"Not many times in your career are you able to give a speech that says exactly what you believe and exactly what you're going to do to everybody who's going to be influenced by what you're doing," Correll says. "I didn't realize it was such a big deal, but the people of Georgia-Pacific were so thirsty for leadership that the speech became known as the 'seven points of light.' They actually hung it on their walls."

Correll wrote the speech himself, working on his computer at home at night for more than two weeks. "I knew it had to say what I believed. I knew it was going to change a lot of these people. They deserved to know what the new rules were."

He began by reassuring the audience that he had no intention of making G-P like Mead or Weyerhaeuser, his former employers — "We are a far better company than either of those places I worked before. If I thought that they were so wonderful, I would have stayed."

Then he quickly outlined the principles that guide his business philosophy:

1. The shareholder owns the company, and we work for him.
2. Cash drives the system.
3. The customer buys our products, and he sets the quality level.
4. Cost is the key.
5. There is value in size.
6. People really make the difference.
7. You earn the right to grow.

Correll told the audience they would be held accountable for understanding such concepts as return on capital and cost of capital. He also said G-P needed to admit it did not have a quality reputation in pulp and paper and that the company must change it. He said everyone has the right to be involved in the decision-making process of the business.

"I have never been in a mill that was clean, had a good safety record and had employees who would talk to you about their jobs that was not also profitable," he said.

At the end of his passionate, 47-page speech, Correll said, "Well, folks, that's me, and that is what I believe." The response was electrifying. As applause rang out, Correll returned to his seat next to Chairman Marshall Hahn. The ever-impish Hahn leaned over and said, "Well, I wish to hell you'd told them what you really thought!"

Correll's speech sent shock waves through the management ranks of Georgia-Pacific, at a time when the company was rife with internal competition between the building products division and the pulp and paper division.

"I think people realized after that that I wanted us to compete with other pulp and paper companies and didn't care whether we were bigger or smaller than the building products division," he says. "More than that, we said we're going to concentrate on costs and returns. We're going to learn how to manage a balance sheet as well as income statements."

Correll's speech had a long-term impact on the company. "It was just incredible," says Michael Burandt, who later became president of North American consumer products. "I remember turning to somebody and saying, 'If this guy can get across half of what he believes in for this organization, he's going to change the organization.'

"Pete was the kind of guy who could get you very motivated about the organization, about yourself, about your opportunity, about where you were going," Burandt says. "You wanted to follow him. I said, 'I'm going to jump in with this guy. I really believe in what he's doing.' I wanted to hook up with him because I felt he had tremendous vision. And, also, he had tremendous fortitude. He was a fighter. He was a guy who could get to the top and be a great leader."

CHAPTER SIX

Moving

Closer

to the

Consumer

As Pete Correll prepared to take over Georgia-Pacific, he encountered some eye-opening truths. He found three major issues that required immediate attention: the environmental responsibility, employee safety and financial health of the company. Correll faced the fact that the corporation was merely paying lip service to environmental matters. In safety, Georgia-Pacific ranked about the same as other forest products companies, which Correll found totally unacceptable. Even into the 1990s, the macho image lingered for people who believed "you weren't a real mill person unless you were missing a finger or two." And the company was saddled with huge debts from the Great Northern Nekoosa acquisition at a time when pulp and paper prices had plummeted. Correll examined the company minutely.

By the mid-1990s, he had to evaluate everything and everyone. "Nothing was to be taken for granted," he says. "Never again would you hear: 'We do it that way because we've always done it that way.'"

Throughout the review process, he says, "I was in shock. We had said for years how lean and mean we were. Then we found out we were neither. I remember staring at a graph of financials, horrified, saying, 'Can this really be so?'" Overhead costs were $250 million to $350 million higher than they should have been, and the company was still following the old philosophy of running its machines full-bore.

"The old conventional wisdom in the industry was to run all-out at full capacity and if you still didn't make money, increase capacity." Correll says. "Much of what we did was a little like those old jokes about the two back-country boys who buy watermelons from farmers for two dollars, take them into the city and

Pete Correll, left, took over the helm of Georgia-Pacific in 1993 and immediately took steps to improve the company's safety and environmental records while improving the bottom line. His efforts can be seen in the improved operations of plants like the paper mill at Toledo, Oregon, right, which has made huge strides in safety as well as efficiency.

sell them for one dollar. When they notice that they're not making any money, their solution is to buy a larger truck."

The ultimate strategy that Correll adopted to get out of the hole was "to do what we do better than anybody."

After he became chairman and CEO in 1993, Correll made operational excellence one of the company's primary goals. Correll set other tough goals for the company as well: improving safety and G-P's environmental stewardship. And he made it a priority to communicate with all employees as they worked together toward these goals, taking the time to visit personally with employees at all levels of the company — in "town hall" meetings at mills and over lunch — and improving internal communications vehicles.

THE MILL IMPROVEMENT PROCESS

Correll analyzed the data and calculated how much money Georgia-Pacific needed to make in order to earn its cost of capital. He was stunned to realize G-P was earning $700 million less than it needed. He called a meeting of his management team and invited consultants from McKinsey & Co. The McKinsey team included James Balloun, who went on to become chairman and CEO of Atlanta-based National Service Industries and a member of G-P's board of directors.

The result of the meeting was the Mill Improvement Program, which created teams at participating mills that would go from department to department, examining every process and asking the question "What if everything at the mill performed not at full capacity but at its *optimum* capacity, what would happen?"

David J. Paterson, executive vice president of pulp and paperboard, describes the importance of not looking at what a mill has done in the past, but examining its theoretical limits for cost and throughput performance. "That analysis forces the mill to look at the manufacturing process differently and to stretch more because they see what really is possible," he says.

The biggest revolution was the sea-change in Georgia-Pacific's deeply held philosophy of running its mills full-bore, then trying to sell whatever they produced. The new process that Correll wanted was a 180-degree change: running to demand, that is, producing only what the company knew it could sell. Adopting this attitude meant trying to dispel another industry myth, that the last ton of production is the most profitable. In fact, Correll discovered, the opposite was true. To keep the mills running (to produce the last ton), wood fiber might have to be hauled farther, driving up the cost, not lowering it. Energy and chemical costs also increased incrementally with the last ton.

Running to demand meant mill downtime when inventories reached their targets or machine "slow-back." The change was shocking in a company that long prided itself on running its machines *over* their capacity.

Pete Correll inaugurated the Mill Improvement Program, which created teams that go from department to department, asking, "What if everything at the mill performed not at full capacity but at its *optimum* capacity, what would happen?" One of the results was a change in G-P's long-held philosophy of running its mills full-bore, then trying to sell what it made. Correll wanted to run on demand — producing only what the company knew it could sell. He had to dispel the industry myth that the last ton of production is the most profitable.

The Mill Improvement Program, developed as part of the company's long-running Economic Value Added program, reduced pulp and paper mill costs by $320 million over five years, from 1994 to 1999, while adding 1,000 tons per day to the company's mill capacity.

By squeezing costs and boosting efficiency, the company cut overhead costs by $300 million in 1996 and 1997, including a painful round of layoffs. And Pete Correll was just getting started.

MAKING GEORGIA-PACIFIC SAFER

Clint Kennedy, Pete Correll's first and closest friend at Georgia-Pacific, recalled the company's historic safety standards with a personal story. A native of Zachary,

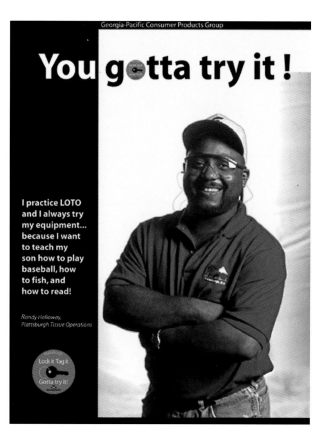

You gotta try it !

I practice LOTO and I always try my equipment... because I want to teach my son how to play baseball, how to fish, and how to read!

Randy Holloway, Plattsburgh Tissue Operations

Lock it Tag it
Gotta try it!

The Brunswick Mill, opposite, produces enormous reels of fluff pulp, which is used to make filters, diapers and other sanitary products. This 18-ton reel contains enough fluff pulp to produce a million diapers. Pete Correll has made safety one of the top priorities at G-P, leading the company to the top of the list with the best safety record in the industry. This recent safety poster, featuring a testimonial from a Plattsburgh, New York, employee, is on display in all of G-P's paper mills.

Louisiana, attending Louisiana State University, Kennedy got a summer job at the Port Hudson mill, where he later launched his G-P career.

"In those days, we weren't very safe, just like we weren't very environmentally conscious," Kennedy said in an interview for this book. "It wasn't that we didn't care about our employees. I think management and the employees thought getting hurt was just part of the deal. If you went to work for a paper mill, there were going to be some accidents. I was working at Port Hudson in college. I worked in the wood yard. A log fell on my leg, and I got hurt and missed about three days of work. I had a lost-time accident as a summer employee. That would be totally, completely unacceptable at Georgia-Pacific today. But nobody thought anything about it then. Every day, we saw the ambulance leaving the mill."

That all changed under Correll, Kennedy said. "Today, if somebody breaks a safety rule that endangers someone else, they get fired."

Correll credits Ron Hogan, former G-P president and vice chairman, with starting the company's SafetyFirst program. "When I took over as president," Correll says, "Ron and I were saying we were going to be the best in safety. I had always believed that safety is

one of the things that management and the hourly people always agree on. Nobody wants anybody to get hurt. We kind of launched that as a rallying cry."

It worked. For the last seven years of the 1990s and again for 2000, the American Forest and Paper Association honored Georgia-Pacific for having the best safety record in the industry. "We originally started with the goal to be in the upper quartile," Correll says, "but as we got into it, I realized that was a lousy goal. We decided we had to be the best."

Richard Benedetti, a veteran West Coast executive for Georgia-Pacific, says Correll doesn't take enough credit for the advances G-P has made in safety. "In the 35 years I've been with G-P, I am most proud of what has been done in safety," Benedetti says. "We had safety before, but Pete Correll is the person who made it a culture and the most important thing we do. Pete has saved lives and stopped people from being crippled. This is a legacy for Pete Correll, and what better legacy would you want than saving lives?"

Fortune magazine picked up on G-P's safety success story in an article in 1997 that said, "For the past four years Georgia-Pacific has recorded the best safety record in the industry. Fully 80 percent of its plants operated last year without any injuries at all. Best of all, nobody died anywhere. The company's mill in Brunswick, Georgia, a vast, hot, clamorous place that produces more fluff pulp (the stuff in disposable diapers, among other things) than anyplace else in the world, now records injuries of 0.7 per 100 workers annually. According to OSHA, that is about one-third the injury rate at an average bank — a place where

With the hiring of Lee Thomas, Pete Correll made important government contacts that thrust him onto a national stage. He participated in a regional conference on the economy with President Bill Clinton in 1995. In addition, Correll took a leadership role in Atlanta on such issues as traffic and changing the state flag. Correll also continued his internal push for safety and for eight years in a row, G-P was the safest company in the forest products industry.

the scariest piece of machinery around is most likely a photocopier."

Fortune noted that an important element in G-P's safety strategy was using humor to get the message across. As an example, the magazine mentioned Wilson "Safety Elvis" Pittman, an employee at the Brunswick mill who bears a keen resemblance to the King of Rock 'n' Roll and sings "Don't step on my steel-toed shoes."

Safety, Correll maintains, is the biggest predictor of outstanding operational performance. "I've always believed that if you could manage safety, you could manage an operation, because the skills it takes to manage safety are the same skills used to manage cost and production. I think we've proven that to be true. If you look at our cost performance and our production performance, they've followed our safety performance."

Tragically, Kennedy — who went on to become

one of Georgia-Pacific's most passionate advocates for safety, efficiency and workplace diversity — lost his life in an accident at his home in the fall of 2000, when he was just 51. An all-terrain vehicle he was loading into his truck fell and killed him. The loss sent Correll reeling, and in subsequent talks about safety, he brought up Kennedy's death and urged employees to be safe on their own time as well as at work.

After eight years as the safest company in the forest products industry, the year 2000 saw a sudden slip in Georgia-Pacific's safety performance, although it remained the industry's safest company. The effort to increase the safety of G-P employees has always been personal to Correll, and at the annual chairman's meeting in Florida in early 2001, he held a sobering safety session for his top managers. He informed them that in the past 12 months, eight G-P employees — who had been with the company from as little as three weeks to as much as 29 years — had lost their lives in accidents.

"For the first time since I've been CEO, our safety record did not improve," Correll told the managers. He described each of the employees who were killed, giving a list of the family members who had survived them. "This was a tragic year for the company," Correll said. "But it was a much more tragic year for these children who will grow up without their fathers because we didn't do our job."

Correll played a videotape that included emotional interviews with G-P workers who had seen their friends die on the job. And he recalled a tragedy that happened early in his career at a mill he managed in

Plymouth, North Carolina, when two millwrights were crushed by a huge paper machine roll that had not been properly secured.

"I will never forget the cranes lifting the roll off those two crushed people," Correll said. "And I am never, ever going to forget going to those homes and telling those families that Daddy wasn't coming home because he got killed in a mill I was running because we didn't do our job."

He urged each of the managers to think about how they could make every employee's job safer. "We can stop killing people in this company, and we have to," he said. G-P began an internal "Get Home Safe" campaign with posters featuring children of company employees.

THE GREENING OF GEORGIA-PACIFIC

Correll became chairman in the midst of a rash of lawsuits filed against Leaf River, the former Great Northern Nekoosa mill in Mississippi, contending the facility was discharging unsafe levels of dioxin into rivers. In addition, Georgia-Pacific still bore the weight of the ancient hatreds of environmentalists dating back to the company's earliest cutting of redwoods in California.

"There was a saying around G-P at the time, 'We're good environmental citizens — we pay our fines on time,'" Correll says. "It became obvious to me that we had to change our behavior and our reputation."

In the early 1990s, the nonprofit Council on Economic Priorities singled out Georgia-Pacific as the worst environmental offender in the forest products industry. The publication *Mother Jones* included Georgia-Pacific on a list it called "The Toxic Ten," saying it had the worst air-permit compliance in its industry and had plants emitting "dangerously high amounts of cancer-causing chloroform into the air of at least four states."

The mindset at Georgia-Pacific had been to hunker down and fight back against environmentalists. "We had prided ourselves in being tough," Correll says, "in thinking, 'You spit across that line and we'll fight.' And we fought. But I ultimately concluded that this was the wrong approach. In many cases, environmentalists' and the public's concerns were based more on fear than on the facts, but I knew we could do more to address those fears. You have to fight things like the dioxin litigation, but you should not fight things like citizens' concerns about the air quality and the water quality and how lands are managed in this country. You ought to work out the solution as a participant."

Correll wanted to change but had no idea where to start. He didn't know a single environmentalist. He hired a headhunter to help him hire either a former Environmental Protection Agency administrator or deputy administrator. As it turned out, the headhunter did not even need to look outside Atlanta.

"We interviewed four or five people," Correll recalls. "Lee Thomas was head and shoulders above anybody else. So we hired him. As it turned out, I stumbled onto one of the most talented executives I've ever met in my life."

Thomas, who had served four years as EPA

administrator under President Reagan, had moved to Atlanta to head the environmental arm of a large engineering firm, Law Engineering and Environmental Services. As it turned out, he had a small-town retail background similar to Correll's. His family had run a general retail business in Ridgeway, South Carolina, for a century.

"Lee was universally regarded in Washington as a straight shooter, a guy who was trying to do his damnedest to do the right thing. He brought a lot of credibility to G-P, and we started down this track together," Correll says.

Thomas joined G-P and eventually rose to the position of executive vice president, consumer products. With Thomas on board, Georgia-Pacific began to put measures in place to track environmental progress and began issuing report cards to tell the public exactly where G-P's environmental efforts stood. Then G-P faced the moment of truth: the Georgia-Pacific mill at Monticello, Mississippi, was about to violate its environmental permit.

"I got a call one afternoon that the lagoons were filling up at Monticello," Correll recalls. "They said, 'It's rained a lot in Mississippi, and we can't release any more without violating our permits. We're going to go ahead and release, and we'll go to the state and get an exclusion.'"

The Monticello mill, which Marshall Hahn had acquired from the St. Regis Corporation in 1984, was the gem of Georgia-Pacific's mills. The company had invested $300 million in it.

Correll listened to the caller from Monticello and said, simply: "Shut it down. Shut it down immediately. Do not violate your permit."

The order reverberated throughout the corporation.

"There's nothing that we ever did to let people know how serious we were that was as powerful as that simple statement, 'Shut it down,'" Correll says. "With that one decision, G-P gained credibility as a responsible corporate citizen that ought to be part of the debate on environmental issues."

With the help of Thomas, Correll was invited to join President Clinton's Council on Sustainable Development and joined the board of The Nature Conservancy. "Pete felt we really needed to establish a new sense of direction for the company that really got us out in front of the environmental issues," Thomas says. "He felt we should take more of a leadership position, as opposed to just reacting to regulations. He said he had never really sat down with any environmentalists and had an interest in doing that. He got to know the leaders of the major national environmental organizations."

These relationships resulted in a groundbreaking development in late 1994, when Georgia-Pacific entered a remarkable agreement with The Nature Conservancy, selecting more than 21,000 acres of land along the Lower Roanoke River in eastern North Carolina to be jointly managed and protected by G-P and the Conservancy.

"To have a forest products company and an independent conservation organization make a commitment to manage forest lands together is truly unprecedented," said Secretary of the Interior Bruce

Georgia-Pacific agreed with the National Wild Turkey Federation to combine wild turkey management with forest management activities on 6.2 million acres of forestland in North America. "Our intent is not only to protect the environment but to recognize that the air and water we're using are not ours.

We're just borrowing them, and it's our responsibility to take care of them."

A truck heads out from a
Georgia-Pacific distribution
division facility with a wide
variety of products for
customers. G-P went through
several money-losing years
trying to revamp distribution
before bringing in Ronnie Paul
to stabilize the operation.
This truck carries gypsum
joint compound, Blue Ribbon
oriented strand board and
Georgia-Pacific plywood
siding, 2x4 lumber and roll
roofing.

Babbitt of the project. The program generated nationwide publicity and led to a series of presentations at the Harvard Business School by Executive Vice President John Rasor of G-P and The Nature Conservancy's president, John Sawhill. "These organizations are combining their core competencies to devise a unique approach to resource and business management," says professor James E. Austin, head of the Harvard Business School's Initiative on Social Enterprise.

Georgia-Pacific's new environmental stewardship went beyond Correll's participation with environmental groups. The company set up the Environmental Policy Council, which established a long-term strategy in 1994. "Our intent is not only to protect the environment but to recognize that the air and water we're using are not ours. We're just borrowing them, and it's our responsibility to take care of them — and to ensure our employees know it," Thomas says.

In the mid-1990s, as Thomas moved up the ladder to take on more and more responsibilities, becoming Correll's right-hand man in the acquisitions of Unisource and Fort James, the company needed a new executive vice president to oversee the environmental program, government affairs and communications. James E. Bostic Jr., the company's highest-ranking African-American, who previously had served as group vice president of communication papers, was named to the position.

Bostic grew up poor in South Carolina and was only the fourth black student to attend Clemson University. Although he met with some resistance — some white students tossed bread at him in the cafeteria — he eventually became Clemson's first black Ph.D. graduate, in chemistry. He won a White House Fellowship, where he served with another up-and-coming young black man — Colin Powell, then a major in the U.S. Army. From the White House, Bostic moved to the U.S. Department of Agriculture, rising to the position of deputy assistant secretary. After President Jimmy Carter took office, Bostic returned to South Carolina to work for Riegel Textiles Corp., in the disposable diaper division.

When former CEO Bob Pamplin bought Riegel in 1985, he immediately sold off the diaper business to cover his purchase costs. Georgia-Pacific was the buyer and welcomed Bostic's talents. Bostic moved through a number of positions of increasingly higher responsibility at G-P. In 1994, he suffered a debilitating stroke — from a blood clot in an artery. It took him a year to recover, but he bounced back and eventually was elected an executive vice president, becoming an important emissary from the company.

THE DISTRIBUTION DEBACLE

One of Correll's most important early challenges came in 1994 as Georgia-Pacific realized it had to make drastic changes in an area in which it had long taken great pride: the building products distribution division.

G-P's distribution division was as close to a sacred cow as the company had. The first distribution center was in Chicago, headed by Owen Cheatham's brother Julian. The division grew under the leadership of

William Hunt. Bob Pamplin gave Hunt 36 hours to invent a new distribution system, and he did, creating wholesale centers for the distribution of building materials. Each of them was an independent profit center — basically an entrepreneurial operation that could be run by one of G-P's mavericks as a stand-alone business.

In the 1960s, with the explosion of Southern pine plywood, Stan Dennison joined G-P to take over distribution in the Southeast. He made sure each major city was covered, then decided which smaller markets to enter, based on growth patterns. Dennison added lumber to the centers, and G-P eventually bought up the warehouses of U.S. Plywood.

In 1967, Owen Cheatham wrote in the company magazine, *Growth*, "We have now developed our marketing system to include 98 distribution centers (with more to come), strategically located throughout the USA, plus 54 sales groups abroad. By doing this, we make the maximum use of the timber owned and harvested by our company, always one of our major goals."

In 1979, the world suddenly changed. Bernie Marcus and Arthur Blank created The Home Depot, which became a fast-growing chain of huge stores filled with lumber, hardware, fixtures and accessories that not only revolutionized the way Americans bought building products but boosted the nation's growing passion for do-it-yourself home repair and renovation.

The Home Depot was a runaway success, rapidly replacing the mom-and-pop lumberyards that for decades had been Georgia-Pacific's bread-and-butter customers. G-P's distribution system suddenly was out

A Georgia-Pacific employee at the Claxton, Georgia, sawmill works at a lumber stacker. G-P uses computer-based optimization techniques to determine how a log should be cut in order to maximize the amount of useable lumber from that log.

Trucks line up at a distribution center to load a variety of products for swift delivery to retailers and other customers. A distribution center yard is set up with stacks of specific products, opposite. A truck moves from one stack to the next as forklifts quickly load the proper products in the specific quantities for that shipment.

of whack with the new reality.

"The distribution division was the sales engine of the company," says Don Glass, who grew up in the division and later became president of The Timber Company. "It became the model for distributing building products in the country up until the mid-1980s. When The Home Depot got into the business in 1979, it was the beginning of the change of the model for distributing products. On comes the 'big box' retailer. They were building their own distribution centers."

Lowe's rose up to compete with The Home Depot and big box retailing grew more powerful and gained more market share, Glass recalls, "it became clear that the casualties out of that change in the supply chain were our primary customers, the mom-and-pop retailers." G-P lost thousands of retail lumber company customers over a decade as they closed, he says.

The rapid changes in the market forced G-P into a dramatic rethinking of the value proposition in distribution. Over the years, the company had developed approximately 160 distribution centers, which became fiercely independent operations selling G-P's building products as well as goods from other companies. The centers were homegrown businesses, each one generating sales between $40 million and $100 million a year in the early 1990s. The local manager did everything from play golf with customers to collect past-due bills.

As Georgia-Pacific began to examine its options, it brought in consultants from McKinsey & Company and brainstormed a radical redesign of the entire distribution channel to take cost out of the system.

The options, Glass recalls, were to shrink the distribution system or totally change the business model. But Georgia-Pacific had never been a company to shrink.

"That was the problem," Glass says. "Nobody wanted to pony up and say, 'shrink's the right thing to do.' No, we thought we had to find a fix."

The company decided to replace the 160 independently run distribution centers with two mega-sales call centers, in Atlanta and Denver, and to use information systems to reduce the costs. The plan would include building massive new distribution centers — 750,000-square-foot warehouses without walls, using a hub and spoke system to handle the same volume for distribution while removing costs from the system.

The change proved to be a disaster. G-P put the new plan into effect in the South first, and problems began to surface immediately. Using technology to drive the new process, orders were taken in call centers and loads were scheduled outside the sales organization. Customers didn't even know when they would receive their shipments.

"We did not have the systems to recognize that when you had a billing error, it needed to be handled promptly and locally," Glass says. "All of those functions got disconnected when we went to this centralized system. It was a mess."

The new system overlooked the importance of the distribution center as a separately run business. "The way the business used to run, when you sold something, everybody knew what was going on. 'Bob needs a load out to John at 2 p.m. Yep, we can do it.' It took eight seconds to make that decision. When it went out

WE'VE BUILT THE NAME AMERICA TURNS TO...

AND BACKED IT WITH THE BROADEST PRODUCT LINE IN THE INDUSTRY.

Lumber. Plywood. Gypsum. Roofing. Paneling. Siding. Insulation. Metal products and more. The kind of product variety and inventory your customers are looking for, whether contractor or consumer.

How do we know? We're America's leading building products manufacturer and supplier, and we've made it our business to know your market. That's why we have more to offer both you and your customers than anyone else.

More products. More in-store displays. More sales support materials. And more nationwide advertising than ever before.

In addition, we have over 150 Distribution Centers and Sales Offices across the country ready to provide mixed load delivery anytime you need it. Or if you prefer, contact your local Distribution Center for mill direct shipment. We give you the choice.

Georgia-Pacific. We're the name America turns to for building materials. Maybe you should, too.

AMERICA BUILDS ON OUR NAME.™

Georgia-Pacific

LUMBER/STRUCTURAL WOOD PANELS
Studs
Dimension Lumber
Pressure Treated Lumber
Plywood
Waferboard
Oriented Strand Board
Particleboard

GYPSUM PRODUCTS/INSULATION
Gypsum Wallboard
Sound Deadening Board
Firestop
Tapes, Textures, Joint Systems Compounds
Foamboard Sheathing
Fiberglass Insulation

ROOFING/METAL PRODUCTS
Standard 3-Tab Shingles
Architectural Shingles
Built-up Roofing
Nails, Screws and Construction Hardware
Remesh and Rebar
Metal Fencing
Metal Roofing Siding

PANELING/SIDING
Real Wood Paneling
Wet Print
Paper Overlay
Plank Panels
Molding
Lumber/Hardboard/Plywood/Vinyl Siding

Georgia-Pacific's building products distribution business has evolved into a full-service network distributing all of the building products under the G-P brand, plus some products manufactured by other companies. These photos show the breadth of G-P's product offerings. The division turned the corner in 1998, with a small profit on sales of $4.3 billion.

the door, everybody could look out the window and watch the truck leave. Guess how the quality check was made — it was, 'You dummy, stop the truck! You've got tongue and groove on the truck! It's the wrong product!'"

"Ultimately," Glass says, "we lost total contact with the customer. We lost our ability to manage the business. It's a locally managed relationship business, and we missed that. We absolutely missed that."

After G-P made the switch to the new system, it not only began losing customers, but it began losing good employees as well. Some of the new people taking orders "didn't know a 2x4 from a sheet of plywood and they certainly didn't know the customer," says CFO Danny Huff.

"Just about anything that could go wrong, went wrong," he says. "We started saving costs. We hired some people to help us with logistics, and they were the wrong people. You ended up not being able to service the customers that you had, which were dwindling. It ended up being a complete debacle.

"We took a business that was making $150 million a year and spent a bunch of capital, and then it lost $150 million a year," Huff says. "That was not tenable."

As Correll watched the new distribution plan roll out, with its glaring problems, he grew increasingly frustrated — and blamed no one but himself. "I made a bad decision," Correll says. "We put the Southeast together and then it started to come apart. I realized we had to do one of two things. We had to go very fast or stop. I made the decision to go very fast — roll the rest of the country in immediately and get the

pain behind us. In retrospect, that was a mistake. I should have stopped. I should have just said, 'This is a bad idea, let's go back to where we were.' It would have been horribly painful, but I could have done it. I didn't do it. So once we were in the mess, we just ended up with capable manager after capable manager failing because they couldn't deal in this new world."

The distribution business was hemorrhaging money, and "it was too broken to sell," Correll says, so he began looking for an aggressive cost manager who knew logistics and building products. He settled on a rough-hewn former G-P employee who had left the fold to spend two decades in the wild and wooly world of Louisiana-Pacific: Ronnie Paul.

Paul is as different from Correll as night is from day, although the CEO pointed out in a speech describing their differences that they were "two boys from the South."

"One launched his career by being good at building and running pulp and paper mills," Correll said. "The other made his name by building and running building products plants. One's beliefs about acceptable behavior were formed in the traditional, button-down-collar, structured, acceptable cultures of the Mead Corporation and the Weyerhauser Company. The other was formed in the entrepreneurial, no-holds-barred culture of Louisiana-Pacific. One was a corporate animal accustomed to rules, structure, playing the game — a master at the corporate world. The other was a freewheeling 'gunslinger,' known for his jet, his phone, his lack of sleep and lack of abiding by the laws of politics: no rules, only results."

It was the right time to recruit Ronnie Paul from L-P. The rough-and-tumble world at Louisiana-Pacific was starting to crumble in Portland. Chairman Harry Merlo, the former G-P executive who left with the original L-P spin-off, resigned in a wild controversy in 1995 involving civil and criminal allegations over defective products and federal air quality violations, plus suits challenging his hiring and treatment of women employees, which were settled prior to trial.

When Correll hired Ronnie Paul, the CEO recalls, "everyone said I was crazy, that we would never work it out; that Ronnie's style and my style were so different. They said we were doomed, but the decision to hire Ronnie has been one of the best I have ever made."

Paul, whose father died when he was just five, grew up in Texas as an adolescent entrepreneur who owned a service station, a garage and a drag racing strip, then went into the trucking business. The only reason he joined Georgia-Pacific in 1971 was to learn how to borrow money.

"I decided I was going to work for them for a year and go back on my own," Paul says. "G-P had the best talent, and they had the courage, and they had the money, and they were doubling the size of the company every five years." But when Georgia-Pacific spun off Louisiana-Pacific in 1973, Paul headed west and stayed for 22 years.

Then Correll asked him to tackle the distribution job. "He said, 'I've decided I want you to go fix it,'" Paul recalls. "So that's what we did."

Paul had a reputation as an aggressive cost manager, but he also believed in incentives. As he worked to reshape the distribution division into a system of 65 centers, he immediately required the centers to hold 7 a.m. meetings every morning — called "Ronnie Paul meetings" — to make sure everyone got an early start. Then when the division finally began to make small amounts of money, he immediately sent a share of it to each distribution employee.

"Ronnie dramatically turned that place around," Correll says. "Then we got it to a level that it was just an okay bad business. We did a major study and concluded the synergies that we all thought existed between our building products business and distribution were another industry myth, that they weren't true."

By 1999, the distribution division returned to profitability, with sales growing $500 million to $4.9 billion and profits improving to $63 million. Georgia-Pacific installed Chuck McElrea as senior vice president in 2000 "with a dream to see if it is possible for Georgia-Pacific to make that a decent business — and that is yet unproven," Correll said at the time. Paul was promoted to executive vice president of wood products and distribution.

The one bright side, Correll says, was that, "We have a big competitive advantage, having gone through this hell. Now our costs are lower than our competitors'."

INTEGRATION

The recovery of pulp and paper from the recession of 1990-1991 was slow, but by 1995, it bounced back as Georgia-Pacific experienced what the company

In 1995, G-P purchased the gypsum wallboard business of Montreal-based Domtar Inc. for $350 million, doubling the size of G-P's gypsum business. Over the next three years, the acquisition generated $950 million in cash. At what was once Domtar's flagship facility in Newington, New Hampshire, above, an employee spreads a gypsum slurry over thick paper sheets; a top sheet will be added further down the line to create a gypsum "sandwich." A Savannah, Georgia, employee holding a clipboard makes a quality control check of a load of ToughRock wallboard made of gypsum, opposite.

would later call the "roman candle recovery" — when G-P's net income tripled compared with the year before — $1.018 billion ($11.29 per share), compared with $310 million ($3.29 per share) in 1994.

Correll, who had been patiently waiting for Georgia-Pacific to digest the debt from the Great Northern Nekoosa acquisition, began his own hunt for companies to bring into the fold and "paint blue" — the phrase coined to describe converting acquired companies to the Georgia-Pacific culture.

He was cautious after Great Northern Nekoosa, which he regarded as a great strategic acquisition even though, as he later acknowledged, G-P paid too much for it and timed it badly because of the subsequent downturn in pulp and paper. In the acquisition deals he would complete as chairman, however, no one ever accused him of paying too much. "I think I learned that it's okay to walk away," he says.

In 1996, Correll purchased the gypsum wallboard business of Montreal-based Domtar Inc. for $350 million, doubling the size of G-P's gypsum business.

Over the next three years, the acquisition generated $950 million in cash.

In 1997, Georgia-Pacific decided to make a run for Fort Howard Corp., based in Green Bay, Wisconsin, which also was being pursued by James River Corp. of Richmond, Virginia. The stakes were much higher at the time for the struggling James River, which had to buy Fort Howard in order to survive. In a merger, James River and Fort Howard created a $7.3 billion consumer products company they named Fort James.

"We were somewhat halfhearted in our effort to buy Fort Howard," Correll recalls. "We weren't desperate, and we passed. In retrospect, that was the right decision, because we bought it cheaper later."

In addition, James River had the stronger consumer brands, which is what G-P really wanted.

In 1998, G-P bought the family-owned CeCorr Inc. of Indianapolis for $276 million when owner Jack Schwartz said he wanted to get out of the business. The purchase enabled G-P to further integrate its corrugated packaging business. Corrugated containers are a key part of G-P's pulp and paperboard group, which includes two main divisions: pulp and bleached paper, and containerboard and packaging. G-P produced three million tons of containerboard a year at four mills, representing approximately 10 percent of U.S. capacity. Approximately 72 percent of the containerboard production is used by G-P's corrugated packaging plants, which manufacture standard corrugated containers, as well as specialty packaging products, such as double- and triple-wall boxes and water-resistant packaging.

In 1999, Correll and Lee Thomas decided to pursue Unisource Worldwide, Inc., the nation's largest distributor of paper products, packaging and janitorial supplies. Correll had previously talked with Unisource CEO Ray Munn about working together but was pressed into action when UGI Corp., a Pennsylvania-based energy company, made a $1.3 billion bid for Unisource. Georgia-Pacific won with a bid of $1.5 billion.

"It was a great acquisition, but the reaction was just horrible," Correll says. "I have never seen so much

In 1999, G-P paid $1.5 billion for Unisource Worldwide, Inc., the nation's largest distributor of paper products, packaging and janitorial supplies. Initially puzzling to industry analysts, the deal made better sense as acquisitions continued to move G-P closer to the consumer.

vehemence explode from the financial community." G-P's stock fell nearly 7 percent on news of the acquisition, closing at $92. "I think what had happened is we had a mixed message coming out of the management team as to what we were going to do, and the market was taken by surprise."

Charles Tufano, formerly vice president of G-P's building products distribution in the West, was named president of Unisource.

Unisource employees, like Hal Wingfield Jr., a warehouse manager for the 400,000-square-foot Unisource facility in Norcross, Georgia, welcomed the G-P takeover. He recalls the first time he saw a group of G-P executives come into the warehouse. "Here comes this bunch of suits, and one guy is smiling and says, 'Hi, I'm Pete. How're you doing?'" Wingfield says. "He's the smilingest guy I've ever seen. Somebody said, 'You'd smile too if you had his money.' But I've seen a lot of people with his money who aren't smiling. He seems to be genuinely happy."

Also in 1999, Georgia-Pacific acquired Wisconsin Tissue, which added to G-P's away-from-home tissue business. Investors were critical of the move because they felt G-P was still a small player in the tissue business. G-P had already begun to enhance its brand strategy, boosting both marketing and advertising for its Angel Soft bath tissue and Sparkle paper towels. But when G-P acquired Fort James in 2000, it had to divest all of the Wisconsin Tissue facilities to secure approval from the Department of Justice.

As Correll surveyed the landscape for ways to change the company, he even discussed selling Georgia-Pacific. He had considered the sale because further consolidation of the industry would have pleased analysts and would have been highly beneficial to G-P shareholders had the company been acquired by a bigger competitor. At another juncture, he considered acquiring commercial building products company Johns Manville, but he could not find the necessary synergies.

As G-P was growing and changing, Fort James was having difficulty merging the cultures of Fort Howard and James River. In 2000, a director who served together with Correll on a corporate board told him that Miles Marsh, the chairman of Fort James, was miserable and might be amendable to a buyout offer. Correll took up the hunt, quickly discussing the deal with Lee Thomas, Danny Huff and other executives.

Michael Burandt, who at the time was senior vice president of packaged products, was about to board a company jet when Correll approached him to talk about the deal: "Pete says, 'Walk with me.' And as we walked around the airplane, he says, 'I'm thinking about taking a pass at Fort James.' And it wasn't three weeks later that he started the process, just like that. Obviously, he had been thinking about this for a long time and was just looking for the right time frame."

Correll quickly made it happen. Georgia-Pacific announced it would acquire Fort James for approximately $11 billion and become the world's largest tissue maker. The acquisition created a dominating stable of consumer products in addition to G-P's rapidly growing Angel Soft, Sparkle and MD brands. The new brands included Quilted Northern, Soft 'n Gentle, Brawny, Mardi Gras, So-Dri, Vanity Fair and Dixie. A key to the deal was bringing Georgia-Pacific's low-cost manufacturing capabilities to Fort James's strong consumer brands and nationwide marketing.

After the Department of Justice reviewed the deal for antitrust considerations, G-P had to divest itself of the away-from-home tissue business it had recently gained with the Wisconsin Tissue acquisition.

Despite the divestiture, G-P did not lose any critical brand names, and it retained all the commercial tissue facilities acquired in the Fort James transaction.

Though the merger of Fort Howard and James River had encountered problems as the two corporate cultures clashed, Correll said he wasn't concerned. G-P was painting Fort James blue. "The clash of cultures ultimately wasn't an issue because our goal

With the acquisition of Fort James Corporation in 2000, Georgia-Pacific became the world's leading tissue maker, with a broad range of popular products, above. G-P welcomed to the fold such new brands as Brawny, Dixie and Quilted Northern.

Like Georgia-Pacific, James River Corporation, opposite, grew largely by acquisition. The horse sculpture below once resided in the headquarters of Crown Zellerbach Corporation. When James River acquired Crown, the horse moved to James River's Richmond, Virginia, headquarters. Georgia-Pacific adopted the tradition, moving the horse to Atlanta, when Georgia-Pacific acquired James River.

In 1969, the Ethyl Corporation in Richmond, Virginia, decided to sell off its original papermaking facilities, including the Albemarle Paper Company's Hollywood Mill. Two Ethyl executives, Brenton S. Halsey and Robert C. Williams, joined forces with a small group of investors to purchase the assets on the James River.

The James River Paper Company started out with 100 employees, manufacturing specialty papers such as blotting and absorbent papers, creped papers, kraft papers, moisture barrier papers and a small line of automotive air and oil filter papers.

Halsey, the chief executive officer, and Williams, the chief operating officer, believed they could revive the previously unprofitable operation. In fact, they launched a

phenomenal enterprise that grew from $4 million in sales to $7 billion by the early 1990s.

The company began to concentrate on specialty automotive air and oil filter papers and grew rapidly through both internal development and acquisition using leveraged financing. Halsey and Williams specialized in buying and turning around poorly performing operations.

In 1973, the company went public with the sale of 165,000 shares of common stock at $12 per share and the parent company was renamed James River Corporation of Virginia.

By its 10th anniversary, James River had made 10 acquisitions — three of which doubled the size of the company. Sales had increased to $298 million.

In 1980, James River purchased the Brown Company from Gulf + Western Industries, Inc., which again doubled the size of the company from $400 million in sales to $800 million. The acquisition enabled James River to enter several new product areas, namely towels and tissues, food and beverage service products, and paperboard packaging — the major base for the company's future growth.

The recession in the early 1980s hammered the specialty paper business. However, the food packaging and consumer products businesses remained steady. Seeking to achieve a balance between cyclical and non-cyclical products — and to gain a major market presence in consumer-related paper products — in 1982, the company purchased the Dixie and Northern assets from American Can Company. Once again, the acquisition doubled the

size of the company; it also included pulp mills in Pennington, Alabama, and Green Bay, Wisconsin.

In 1983, James River purchased American Can's Marathon, Ontario, pulp mill and the pulp and papermaking assets of Diamond International Corporation, which included Vanity Fair tissue. The next year, James River expanded into Europe and was ranked as number one in sales growth in the Fortune 500.

James River acquired Crown Zellerbach Corporation for $1.6 billion in 1986, doubling the size of the company for the sixth time. But as the company moved into the

1990s, it was widely viewed as unfocused. Halsey stepped down as chairman and CEO in 1992 and was succeeded by Williams, who held the top post until 1996. He was succeeded by Miles L. Marsh, who had been chairman and CEO of Pet Food Inc.

When James River acquired Fort Howard in 1997, creating Fort James as the second-largest tissue producer in the world, it brought to the new company strong consumer brands, including Dixie, Nice 'n Soft, Quilted Northern, Vanity Fair and Brawny.

Fort Howard Corporation was founded in 1919 by Austin E. Cofrin, an iron-willed visionary with a grade-school education, in Green Bay, Wisconsin.

Cofrin was raised on a farm in Vermont and got his first job in a paper mill at 16, moving to New York, Philadelphia and London, Ontario, before landing in Green Bay as a mill manager for Northern Paper. At 36, Cofrin was fired in a management shakeup. He rounded up a few investors, found land on the west side of the Fox River and put up a building for a paper machine.

"We are going to do this," Cofrin vowed. "And we are going to do it better than anybody else."

Cofrin's company became one of the largest, lowest-cost tissue producers in the United States. Fort Howard created a competitive advantage by developing a method of recycling waste paper for the production of pulp. The company generated its own power and machined its own equipment.

Cofrin's son, John P. Cofrin, succeeded him as chief executive in 1959. Interested in growth, the younger Cofrin took the company public in 1971. He died three years later and was succeeded by Paul J. Schierl.

In 1983, Fort Howard acquired Maryland Cup for $515.5 million and three years later acquired Lily Tulip, another cup manufacturer, for $322 million. The company had become a diversified industrial giant with 17,000 employees and annual sales of $1.76 billion. But the cup business clashed with Fort Howard's culture.

"In Green Bay, we have an extremely hardworking, aggressive group of people," Schierl said. "That was not the culture of Maryland Cup. Things were considerably more easy-going." Additionally, he said Lily Tulip had been depleted of its talent by a leveraged buyout. "They were dressing her up to sell, but they weren't feeding her very well."

Schierl and other managers joined a Morgan Stanley-led leveraged buyout of Fort Howard for $3.7 billion at $53 per share in 1988, and sold $1.3 billion in junk bonds to help finance the LBO. The company would not earn a quarterly profit again until 1994. In 1989, Fort

From its origins on the Fox River in Green Bay, Wisconsin, left, Fort Howard created some of the better known brands of low-cost tissues, eventually shipping Soft 'n Gentle, Mardi Gras and recycled Green Forest products across the country, opposite. Though it had pioneered the production of tissue from recycled waste paper, Fort Howard had a turbulent history of public and private ownership that culminated in its acquisition by James River in 1997.

Howard sold its cup operations to focus on tissue.

Donald H. DeMeuse succeeded Schierl in 1990 and took Fort Howard public again the next year.

Fort Howard specialized in low-cost tissues, especially for the away-from-home market and consumer markets. Its best-known brands were Soft 'n Gentle tissues, Mardi Gras napkins and Green Forest recycled tissue products. By the late 1990s, the company had 6,800 employees worldwide and was heavily in debt.

DeMeuse retired in 1997 and was succeeded as chairman by Michael T. Riordan, who sold the company within three months.

When James River bought Fort Howard in 1997 to create Fort James, it paid $3.3 billion and assumed $2.4 billion in debt. Riordan was named president, reporting to the new chairman and CEO, Miles L. Marsh, who had held the same posts at James River.

The newly created company, with annual sales of $7 billion, was headquartered in Chicago.

Lee Thomas (standing) and Pete Correll were greeted by cheers and applause as they welcomed Fort James employees to Georgia-Pacific. The employees were pleased to join the well-managed Georgia-Pacific, which had nearly three times the sales of their former company.

is to bring the Fort Howard and James River cultures into the Georgia-Pacific culture. And I think that has gone very well."

The acquisition signified an enormous shift in Georgia-Pacific's focus toward the customer. "We are transforming the Georgia-Pacific asset portfolio by moving up the value chain, focusing on higher margin businesses that are closer to our customers and on our core competencies that will provide greater and more

predictable cash flows," Correll wrote in his letter to shareholders in G-P's 2000 annual report. "We are very excited about the powerful stable of brands that we now manage. The growth of those brands, combined with the sale of some of our commodity businesses, should make this a much different, but most importantly a more valuable enterprise five years from now."

Georgia-Pacific planned to sell off assets that didn't fit its consumer-oriented focus. In April 2001, the company announced it was selling a portion of its pulp and paper business to Domtar Inc., in a transaction valued at $1.65 billion. The assets were G-P's stand-alone uncoated fine paper mills at Ashdown, Arkansas; Nekoosa and Port Edwards, Wisconsin; and Woodland, Maine, as well as associated pulp facilities. Correll said the divestiture would reduce debt while further refining the company's portfolio of assets.

Though Georgia-Pacific's strategy was now more focused, analysts still wondered whether G-P could compete with such skilled marketing giants as Procter & Gamble and Kimberly-Clark. As *Atlanta Journal-Constitution* writer Patti Bond put it, "Can the prince of plywood go toe-to-toe with Mr. Whipple?" Bond wrote that analysts who questioned Correll in New York after the Fort James announcement were worried about G-P "thrusting itself into the ring with consumer powerhouses. Correll fielded question after question about how his company could square off in a marketing arena that has made a household icon of grocer George Whipple and his 'Please, don't squeeze the Charmin' ads."

Correll responded, according to Bond: "I've been somewhat embarrassed…that people don't understand how well we run our tissue business."

"The fact is," Bond wrote, "the company has bragging rights. Georgia-Pacific has steadily taken market share from the top players since it got into the branded tissue business in the late 1980s. One reason is price. Angel Soft bathroom tissue and Sparkle paper towels typically cost less than the top-selling brands." She also attributed the company's growth to "market-

ing smarts," singling out Mike Burandt for consumer tissue sales success and marketing manager Rob Lorys, who "boosted the Sparkle brand with the 'Health Smart' campaign, which gave it an antibacterial spin."

In 2000, to take its full branding message to consumers, Georgia-Pacific adopted a new slogan: "We make the things that make you feel at home." The theme was the result of detailed research into the customers of the big box retailers that have been selling Georgia-Pacific products to the public.

"We wanted a detailed analysis of our major customers, like The Home Depot, Lowe's, Office Max and Wal-Mart," says Sheila Weidman-Farley, vice president of corporate marketing. "Those are the people who are buying our products. And those are the people we call Middle America. More than that, we found they are home-centric people. They are do-it-yourselfers. They spend time at home with their families. Their home is the foundation of their lives. They're positive thinkers. They look for value. They're community-oriented.

"Once we had defined our customer, we determined that no competitor had the breadth of products that we do that are so linked to the American home — from bath tissue, paper towels, Dixie products, disposable tableware and paper for the home office printer to lumber for the decks on the back of the house, plywood, gypsum wallboard and industrial wood products used to make cabinets in the kitchen," Weidman-Farley says. "The home is where we intersect with our target consumer. All of that came together for our strategic brand positioning and the theme."

The theme was rolled out during 2000, with

Country singing star Lee Ann Womack, the spokesperson for the Sparkle brand, performed in 2000 in Atlanta in front of a house built of Sparkle products. The celebration honored Georgia-Pacific's contribution of all paper products used in the 145 Ronald McDonald Houses nationwide.

cable television advertising in 26 markets covering 31 percent of the country's households. Familiarity with Georgia-Pacific rose 46 percent in those markets, and the preference for buying G-P products rose 64 percent, Weidman-Farley says. In 2001, G-P rolled out the campaign nationally, focusing on wholesome family programming on networks and cable viewed by the target consumers.

Correll explained in an interview for this book what he hopes consumers will think about the Georgia-Pacific brand: "They can trust it; it provides very good quality for the dollars they pay. For Middle America, this is the supplier whose brands I can trust. If you drive a pickup truck or van, if you shop at Wal-Mart, The Home Depot or Lowe's, if you stay at the Day's Inn, if you're married, have two kids and those values mean a lot — I want Georgia-Pacific to be associated with that. If I ever go into the Cloister Hotel or the Waldorf Astoria and find a Georgia-Pacific product, I want to be surprised it's there. But if I ever go to a Day's Inn, Holiday Inn or a Hampton Inn and I don't find it, I want to be shocked and wanting an explanation of why it's not there. I want to position this company as the forest products supplier to Middle America."

As Georgia-Pacific moved closer to that demographic, it announced a major NASCAR sponsorship, backing the No. 44 Dodge run by Petty Enterprises and driven by Roy "Buckshot" Jones for the 2001 Winston Cup Series. The program quickly generated favorable publicity for G-P in publications ranging from the *Atlanta Journal-Constitution* to *Southern Living* and drew upwards of 400 customers to each of the

company's hospitality events at the mammoth racetracks. The start of G-P's sponsorship coincided with the 2001 debut of NASCAR race coverage on FOX, later moving to NBC and TNT. The races proved to be more popular than many competing sports events, including some professional golf tournaments and post-season college basketball games.

"It's a very good sport for us to talk to our target consumers," Weidman-Farley says. "It's a branded sport, and that's truly unique. And we were fortunate to link up with Petty Racing, which has a wonderful brand for integrity and honesty."

GEORGIA-PACIFIC: CORPORATE CITIZEN

As he mentored Pete Correll, Marshall Hahn explained the long Atlanta tradition of civic

Georgia-Pacific announced a new NASCAR partnership with Petty Enterprises for the 2001 racing season. G-P became the primary sponsor for the No. 44 Dodge Intrepid R/T driven by Roy "Buckshot" Jones, opposite. The project was spearheaded by the late Clint Kennedy, G-P's executive vice president of pulp and paper at the time. In the photo above, Kennedy (left) joins Buckshot Jones, Richard Petty and Kyle Petty (left to right). Chairman Pete Correll said NASCAR's loyal fans and G-P's customer base were "virtually a perfect match."

Employees in Atlanta swarm over one of six Habitat for Humanity houses they built in 2000-2001, left, proving not only can they sell building products, they know how to use them. Below, Marshall Hahn donated a present for a needy child to the Salvation Army Angel Tree in the Georgia-Pacific lobby in 1992.

Georgia-Pacific encourages its employees to be good corporate citizens in the communities where they live.

Pete Correll, described by one employee as "the smilingest guy I've ever seen," greets an employee at a G-P facility. In 2001, Correll personally spearheaded a fundraising effort among Atlanta CEOs to pay for the restoration of the historic Ebenezer Baptist Church in Atlanta, once the church of the Reverend Martin Luther King Jr.

involvement by CEOs, dating back to the role of Asa Candler, the Coca-Cola founder who served as mayor; Robert Woodruff, the legendary Coca-Cola chairman and philanthropist who was a key force in Atlanta's peaceful desegregation; and Ivan Allen, the business-man-mayor who presided during the Civil Rights era.

Hahn had led the Metropolitan Atlanta Chamber of Commerce and made it clear to his successor that much would be expected of him.

Correll became a key player on groups that tackled some of Atlanta's most important issues. He was chair of the Metropolitan Atlanta Transportation Initiative that addressed Atlanta's problems with traffic gridlock and led to the creation of the Georgia Regional Transportation Authority.

Correll and Jim Bostic were credited with playing pivotal roles in helping Governor Roy Barnes change the Georgia state flag, which featured a large Confederate battle symbol. Many proponents of the flag, which was approved by the state legislature in 1956, argued that it was an attempt to honor the state's Confederate heritage. Opponents, however, argued that it was an act of racial defiance by a legislature opposed to desegregation.

"I called everybody I knew and explained the issue. I was a freshman in high school in Brunswick, Georgia, when they changed the flag, so I knew all the stories about it being the flag of our fathers and grandfathers simply were not true," Correll says. "I remember when they changed the flag and why they changed the flag.

"If I care about something, I try to do something about it. And I did care about this issue. I was embarrassed to fly the state flag in front of our corporate headquarters building because it offended our employees."

Bostic worked directly with the governor in the days leading up to the momentous change, when the legislature adopted a flag that featured small versions of the previous state flags, diffusing the racially charged issue.

Bostic, who became an executive vice president in 2001 and also headed up education issues for the Atlanta Chamber of Commerce, says Georgia-Pacific — in a traditionally white male industry — has made great strides in hiring a more diverse workforce.

"When I came to Georgia-Pacific, having a black person in the management team was new," Bostic says, "and there were not many black people in senior jobs in the company. But that has changed a great deal.

Marshall Hahn made it a big issue for managers to understand how important it was to hire minorities and women in the organization, and Pete has continued that. He is very, very strong in terms of what he believes."

One of the strongest statements on behalf of workplace diversity came from a white Louisianan, Clint Kennedy, who walked into a meeting of top management at Unisource after G-P had acquired the company, and proclaimed, "All I see is middle-aged white guys!"

Correll turned the task of diversifying the

Pete Correll addresses one of the many "town hall" meetings he has held throughout the country to stay in touch with G-P's increasingly diverse workforce and give employees an opportunity to ask him questions about the business. Correll responds candidly and with good humor.

company over to an old friend from Mead, Pat Barnard, who also was elected an executive vice president of G-P in 2001. Barnard, who says she was ignored when she arrived at G-P, just as Correll had been, eventually moved up the ladder to become the company's top human resources officer. Most G-P officers felt it was difficult to recruit women and minorities for small-town posts in places like Crossett, Arkansas, but Barnard reported that an increasing number of young women were willing to try such an assignment because of the chance to develop rapidly in a demanding professional environment inside a community that had changed little since the 1950s.

Few women had made it to the top echelons of Georgia-Pacific. The earliest was Mary McCravey, who was recruited by Robert Pamplin from the University of Georgia Law School in 1948, when the company was still in Augusta. McCravey served as G-P's corporate secretary for most of her career and retired in Portland.

A half-century later, working in an all-male environment on the 51st floor of G-P headquarters, Barnard had learned to survive: "You earn your credibility and respect just like anyone else does, and you become a peer. Now I'm just one of them." Barnard even learned to shoot a gun and hunt along with her fellow officers. "They're a good group of people," Barnard says, "and I'm persistent. They don't see me as a woman executive," she says. "They see me as a G-P executive."

Before Barnard ever came to G-P, she learned an important lesson at Mead from Pete Correll that ironically would work in her favor after she moved to Atlanta. "Pete taught me that you always want to learn how to manage your boss. He taught me how to do that, to manage a person. Now, he's my boss!"

COMMUNITY INVOLVEMENT ACROSS THE BOARD

While Correll and Bostic were involved in top-level civic issues in Atlanta, employees of Georgia-Pacific across the country contributed to their own communities in a wide range of activities that often received financial backing from the company as well.

In 1999-2000, the Georgia-Pacific Foundation invested $7,127,131 in efforts to enhance education, the environment and enrichment of local communities, as well as to support the aspirations of G-P employees. In addition to direct contributions, the Foundation fostered efforts by thousands of employees who gave time and attention to improving their communities. The Foundation invested funds in hundreds of not-for-profit organizations, provided $750,000 in scholarships to children of employees and coordinated community investments.

For example, the Foundation marked its 10-year partnership with the St. Croix International Waterway Commission in Maine with the successful release of 750 adult Atlantic salmon into the St. Croix River.

In Colorado, the Foundation sponsored 15 middle-school teachers to participate in the Keystone Science School, an intensive summer curriculum. More than 50 G-P employees served in a meals-on-wheels program in Virginia during their lunch breaks, with the Foundation contributing $20,000.

In Georgia, more than 200 G-P employee volunteers helped create a "success zone" for 325 students at Atlanta's M. Agnes Jones Elementary School with the one-on-one "Georgia-Pacific Buddy" tutoring program. In Mississippi, G-P employees built homes for Habitat for Humanity. In Connecticut, the G-P Norwalk Mentoring Program motivated students to stay in school. In Louisiana, G-P sponsored the Young Leaders Academy, a rigorous training program for inner-city boys in Baton Rouge.

"Working as one, we are honoring a tradition of commitment and action," Curley M. Dossman Jr., president of the G-P Foundation, said in G-P's 2001 Community Investment Report.

THE TIMBER COMPANY MERGER

The day after Georgia-Pacific announced the Fort James acquisition, it announced it was spinning off its trees to further the move away from its commodity roots. Under the approximately $4 billion deal, Georgia-Pacific spun off its timber-growing arm, The Timber Company, and merged it with Plum Creek Timber Co., based in Seattle, effective in the fall of 2001. The Timber Co., which had been created as a separate operating company with its own stock in 1997, had six million acres, mostly in the Southeast. Shareholders of Plum Creek, Correll said, "received the benefits of investing in a coast-to-coast manager of diversified timber and land assets."

Correll had stunned the industry with the move, declaring that manufacturers didn't have to own timberlands to be competitive. Don Glass, president of The Timber Co., went even further, saying in an interview for this book: "Georgia-Pacific was never really in the tree business. It was always in the fiber consumption business. It was actually in the tree business just to make fiber for its mills."

The creation of The Timber Co. worked well, according to Glass. "At the end of two years, we collectively came to a conclusion that we were able to sell our logs at a higher price on average because we could determine when we wanted to sell them,

The Timber Company welcomed Governor Kirk Fordyce of Mississippi (third from right) to the Pearl River Nursery at Hazelhurst, Mississippi. Joining the governor were (left to right) Doug Sharp, regeneration manager; Ken Woody, nursery manager; John Pait, director of forest productivity; Donald L. Glass, president and CEO of The Timber Company; and Gary A. Myers, vice president of resource management for The Timber Company.

and so take advantage of changes in the market," Glass says. "Conversely, G-P's buyers got better because they were forced to buy more of their wood in the open market. They couldn't just reach across the table when times got tough and say, 'Gee, I ran out of wood at my mill. I'm going to come on our property and buy 50 more loads next week.' I said, 'Sorry you can't do that.' So they had to become more disciplined in their buying. They lowered their wood costs while we raised our sales average, and both sets of shareholders are better off."

The Timber Co. also discovered additional new cash streams coming off the property, including revenues from mineral oil and natural gas leases, as well as revenues from leasing property for optic cables, cell towers and billboards. In addition, the company leases rights to sportsmen, primarily in the South, where they hunt everything from deer to wild turkey. The hunting leases generate $12 million a year in income from 40,000 hunters, who also keep a close eye on the land and report poachers and illegal dumping.

Unleashed from the mills, The Timber Co. intensified its focus on extracting full value from its forest assets and determined that not every acre it owned was best suited for forestry. The company accelerated its taxable land sales program, examining every acre to determine whether it is best suited for forestry or for some other purpose. It would sell higher-use lands or less productive acres and seek better-located, more productive acres. As a result, the company is constantly upgrading the quality of its portfolio, buying and selling approximately 60,000 acres a year and achieving the maximum value for each acre with its best use.

"In 1997," Glass says, "Georgia-Pacific created its first completely new product in over 20 years — the tree. We decided to begin practicing intensive silviculture and focused on obtaining the maximum available for every tree rather than just feeding fiber into G-P mills to keep manufacturing costs low. This was a fundamental shift in how we viewed the forest assets." With a single mindset and intense focus on developing as much value as it could from all aspects of the timberlands — growing trees, optimizing land values and extracting income from minerals and other surface leasing opportunities — G-P believed it could generate significantly more value for the shareholders.

"The creation of The Timber Company signaled a major shift from the integrated model," Glass says. "It made G-P's mills better buyers of logs and users of capital and allowed the forestry professionals to increase returns on the forest assets." The merger of Plum Creek and The Timber Company creates the largest timber company in the U.S. and one with the expertise, resources and diversified holdings to maximize the value of the forest for shareholders.

INTO THE NEW MILLENNIUM

Georgia-Pacific was headed on a new track as it moved into the new century. The company ended the year 2000 with a 20 percent increase in sales to $22.08 billion from $18.42 billion the year before. G-P reported profit of $343 million or $1.94 per share, down from $716 million and $4.07 a share in the prior year. After the Fort James acquisition, the company's debt soared to $16 billion, and G-P was determined to reduce that amount to $9.5 billion within three years.

The Fort James acquisition was clearly the biggest risk of Correll's career — a maverick move in the great Georgia-Pacific tradition as he tried to transform the company by moving more heavily into consumer brands to avoid the troubling commodity cycles that had plagued the company.

"I don't know whether it's maverick or desperation or frustration," Correll says, "but whatever it is, I've convinced myself it's the right thing to do. Not only that, it's the only thing to do."

The move toward the consumer and the spinning-off of timberlands led some Georgia-Pacific employees to grumble that the changes would cause Owen Cheatham to roll over in his grave. Yet Cheatham's last relative on the Georgia-Pacific payroll, Walter Cheatham, disagreed: "I think if Owen was around, he'd be looking for the next deal."

Owen Cheatham himself seemed to answer this question as he reflected on both the past and future of his company in 1967, writing:

"Now, when a Virginia boy with six thousand dollars in the bank and an ambition can get from Maple Valley Farm and be telling a story about a billion-dollar company with 35 billion board feet of timber in just forty years, a story which is fact and not fiction the boy once dreamed about under a tree, well, I just don't think there's much to worry about in our economy, especially when you remember that the men and women of Georgia-Pacific really are just getting started."

Cheatham could say the same about the men and women of today's Georgia-Pacific. Three decades after Owen Cheatham wrote those words about his childhood dreams, Pete Correll found a way to transform Georgia-Pacific by dispelling the ancient myths of the forest products industry and moving Georgia-Pacific closer to its customers. G-P now makes what consumers want to buy instead of trying to sell them what the company wants to make. As Correll shook the company to its core, he told employees: "We are changing the most important thing: we are changing the way we think."

Georgia-Pacific now enters the twenty-first century with an enormous stable of popular consumer products, as "a brand-new G-P." And as Cheatham wrote and Correll confirmed, such dramatic progress and transformation is only possible because the men and women of Georgia-Pacific believe it is.

No other company matches Georgia-Pacific's breadth of products linked to the American home — from bath tissue, paper towels, Dixie products, disposable tableware and paper for the home office printer to lumber for the decks on the back of the house, plywood, gypsum wallboard and industrial wood products used to make cabinets in the kitchen. In 2000, G-P adopted a new slogan to reflect its position: "We make the things that make you feel at home."

Acknowledgments

Five strong men have led Georgia-Pacific. I was fortunate to meet three of them: Robert E. Flowerree, a gracious gentleman who shaped the company during its great surges of growth; T. Marshall Hahn Jr., the scholar turned businessman who brought the company out of a brutal recession; and A. D. "Pete" Correll, a modern executive who embodies the maverick tradition of the company's founders. Correll not only transformed Georgia-Pacific, but also provided powerful leadership in changing Atlanta and Georgia for the better.

The pioneers of Georgia-Pacific had enormous vision and the courage to bring it to life. I was privileged to speak with members of the founding family: Celeste Wickliffe Cheatham, Kenneth R. Kennerly, Alyce Cheatham and Walter B. Cheatham II.

Virtually everywhere I visited, from sprawling mills to towering offices to lovely homes, I encountered an appreciation of wood as a thing of beauty apart from its practical role in G-P's fortunes. I saw stunning wood-paneled rooms in the homes of Marion L. Talmadge and Davis K. Mortensen. I thank them for their memories.

I am especially indebted to John R. Ross, author of *Maverick: The Story of Georgia-Pacific*, published on the occasion of the company's 50th anniversary. His interviews, research and observations were invaluable.

Stephen K. Jackson was most helpful in setting me on my path to discovery, Danny W. Huff combined keen insight with a reverence for the past and

Donald L. Glass gave me a college education in one session. Hoping that I have not omitted anyone, I would also like to thank the many others who shared their thoughts, stories and good humor, including Patricia A. Barnard, Dick Benedetti, Don Blank, James E. Bostic Jr., Michael C. Burandt, Max Braswell, Stanley S. Dennison, Edward B. Fitzpatrick III, Harvey C. Fruehauf Jr., Richard V. Giordano, Richard A. Good, Edythe M. Gukenberger, Robert D. Hanry, Kenneth F. Khoury, Stephen E. Macadam, Mark R. Matheny, David A. Odgers, David J. Paterson, Ronald L. Paul, John F. Rasor, Daniel J. Renbarger, Lee M. Thomas and Hal Wingfield Jr.

I was honored to interview Clint M. Kennedy, who was an important agent for change within the company, prior to his untimely death.

I could not have attempted the book without the help and guidance of Sheila Weidman-Farley and the unfailingly friendly people who work with her, especially Naomi Anderson, who may be G-P's most enthusiastic NASCAR fan. Go #44! Corporate photographer James F. Robinson deserves thanks for the time he spent helping to find the beautiful images that bring this story to life. I also appreciate Francis L. Giknis Jr. and Patrick Hodges for accompanying me on a tour of G-P mills during an Arkansas heat wave. I thank you all.

Doug Monroe
October 2001

Timeline

1927

Owen R. Cheatham purchases a wholesale lumber-yard in Augusta, Georgia, for $12,000. The company he incorporates on September 22 as Georgia Hardwood Lumber Company will later become known as Georgia-Pacific Corporation.

1932

Cheatham hires his first salesman and develops an export market for Georgia Hardwood in Europe.

1934

Georgia Hardwood moves its corporate offices from the lumberyard to the Southern Finance Building in downtown Augusta. At the time of the move, the office staff numbers six including Cheatham. Cheatham hires Robert B. Pamplin as the new bookkeeper.

1937

Julian Cheatham, younger brother of Owen, joins the company.

1938

The company owns and operates five sawmills in the South.

1941

World War II begins. Georgia Hardwood becomes the largest supplier of lumber to the U.S. armed forces and earns the Army/Navy "E" Award for outstanding service in the war effort. The company acquires additional mills and lumberyards in the Carolinas, Alabama and Mississippi between 1941 and 1945 to keep up with wartime demand.

1943

James Buckley joins the company to head business in the East and convinces Cheatham to add plywood and lumber from Douglas fir in the Northwest to the company's product offerings.

1947

Georgia Hardwood acquires its first West Coast facility, Bellingham Plywood Company, at Bellingham, Washington, for approximately $1.1 million. Cheatham sells 100,000 shares of common stock to help pay for the acquisition. He adds a wholesale distribution warehouse and distributing yard to the Bellingham operation. After the acquisition, Georgia Hardwood employees number 750 and sales total $24 million.

1948

The company, renamed Georgia-Pacific Plywood and Lumber Company, acquires a controlling interest in Washington Veneer, with two plywood mills at Olympia, Washington, and a controlling interest in Springfield Plywood Company of Springfield, Oregon.

1949

Georgia-Pacific stock is listed on the New York Stock Exchange for the first time on January 27. The company acquires a hardwood plywood plant at Savannah, Georgia. Sales reach $37 million.

1950

Georgia-Pacific formalizes the division of the company into geographic "zones" — Eastern, Southern, Midwestern and Western — responsible for selling, purchasing and manufacturing.

1951

Georgia-Pacific acquires C. D. Johnson Lumber Company of Toledo, Oregon, gaining 66,000 acres of timberlands and a sawmill for $16.8 million. Reflecting its shifting focus, the company drops the word lumber from its name, becoming Georgia-Pacific Plywood Company.

1952

Robert E. Floweree, who had been working at C. D. Johnson, joins Georgia-Pacific to run the Toledo mill.

1953

Georgia-Pacific headquarters move from Augusta, Georgia, to Olympia, Washington.

1954

Georgia-Pacific headquarters move again, from Olympia, Washington, to Portland, Oregon. Pamplin initiates a new acquisition strategy, borrowing $12 million to purchase 19,000 acres of timberland and a sawmill near the Toledo operation, liquidating much of the older timber to repay the loan and reforesting the land. The company also acquires 23,000 acres known as the Oregon-Mesabi tracts, making the deal over a single weekend.

1955

Earnings triple over the previous year's figure.

1956

Georgia-Pacific acquires Coos Bay Lumber Company of Coos Bay, Oregon, for $70 million and Hammond Lumber Company in northern California for $75 million. Together, the acquisitions include 8 billion feet of timber on 247,000 acres and help to double the company's plywood production, but the company incurs heavy debt. The company name changes again to Georgia-Pacific Corporation. A new sales distribution system is implemented, including the addition of 10 distribution centers for a total of 40. Sales reach $121 million.

1957

Robert Pamplin is elected president of G-P. Robert Flowerree leads the company into the pulp and paper business with the construction of a $20 million kraft pulp and linerboard mill at Toledo, Oregon. Using dynamic conservation methods, G-P reforests more acreage than it logs this year.

1959

Georgia-Pacific acquires Booth-Kelly Lumber Company of Springfield, Oregon, for $93 million. G-P also enters the chemicals business, manufacturing its own resins at Coos Bay, Oregon. Distribution centers total 60.

1960

Georgia-Pacific acquires W. M. Ritter Lumber Company in the Southeast, including timberlands with oil, coal and other mineral deposits, bringing G-P's timberland ownership to a total of one million acres. G-P stock hits 59 3/4, up from just 2 1/4 in 1953. Owen Cheatham suffers a stroke; though Cheatham remains chairman and CEO, Pamplin now runs the company.

1961

New paper converting facilities in Washington, California, Iowa, Illinois and Arkansas boost the company's paper production. Flowerree builds the company's first corrugated container plant, at Olympia, Washington, and acquires National Box and Specialty Company of Sheboygan, Wisconsin, and Oshkosh Corrugated Box Manufacturing Company of Oshkosh, Wisconsin. G-P employees now number 11,197.

1962

Georgia-Pacific pays $125 million for Crossett Lumber Company of Crossett, Arkansas, including 565,000 acres of timberlands. The company adds a corrugated container plant at Modesto, California, and a grocery bag and sack plant at Toledo, Oregon. Sales reach $324 million, generating $19 million in profits.

1963

Georgia-Pacific leaps into the tissue business, acquiring two well-established tissue manufacturers: Vanity Fair Paper Mills in Plattsburgh, New York, and Puget Sound Pulp and Timber Company of Bellingham, Washington, including its Hopper Paper Division and MD tissue brand. Unable to obtain the Vanity Fair brand name, G-P begins manufacturing tissue under the name "Coronet." G-P also acquires St. Croix Paper Company of Woodland, Maine, and Fordyce Lumber Company of Fordyce, Arkansas. After much experimentation, G-P became the first company to successfully manufacture plywood made from Southern pine, at Fordyce, Arkansas.

1964

Georgia-Pacific creates a chemicals division to oversee the expansion of that business, which includes a new chlorine and caustic soda plant at Bellingham, Washington and a sodium chlorate and sulfuric acid plant.

1965

Georgia-Pacific acquires a steady supply of gypsum wallboard for its 84 distribution centers with the purchase of Bestwall Gypsum Company of Paoli, Pennsylvania. The company expands paper and chemical facilities as well, acquiring specialty paper manufacturer George La Monte & Son of Nutley, New Jersey.

1966

Georgia-Pacific adds 13 new manufacturing plants and expands five existing facilities. It acquires from National Polychemicals, Inc., the Lufkin, Texas, and Conway, North Carolina, chemical facilities. A new chip export facility added at Coos Bay, Oregon, begins to export chips to Japan.

1967

Georgia-Pacific breaks ground on its first company-owned headquarters building in Portland, Oregon. The company acquires Kalamazoo Paper Company of Kalamazoo, Michigan. G-P creates a chemical sales division to market its chemicals to outside customers. Robert Pamplin succeeds Owen Cheatham as chairman of the board.

1968

Georgia-Pacific begins constructing a large chemical refining complex in Plaquemine, Louisiana, and continues to grow with the addition of more timberlands and plywood plants. Sales exceed $1 billion for the first time.

1969

Wrapping up a decade of tremendous growth, the company acquires a kraft pulp mill at Port Hudson, Louisiana, completes a new gypsum plant at Buchanan, New York, and adds 11 new sawmills. It also donates California redwood groves valued at more than $6 million to The Nature Conservancy.

1970

The company opens its completed corporate headquarters building. The distribution division has grown to include 105 distribution centers across the country.

1972

Georgia-Pacific faces scrutiny from the Federal Trade Commission concerning its share of the Southern pine plywood market. G-P spins off $305 million in assets as Louisiana-Pacific Corporation, pursuant to a settlement with the FTC.

1973

The company acquires redwood timberlands and sawmills at Fort Bragg, California, from Boise Cascade. The company announces a $1 billion, five-year capital investment program. Sales reach $2.2 billion.

1975

The company acquires Exchange Oil & Gas Corporation of New Orleans, Louisiana, to assure the natural gas supply for the methanol plant in Plaquemine, Louisiana. Completed construction of plywood plants in Alabama, Georgia and South Carolina. Operated more than 140 distribution centers and more than 200 plants and mills. Robert Pamplin names Robert Flowerree president. G-P employees now number 33,500.

1976

Georgia-Pacific dives deeper into the building products market, announcing plans for a roofing manufacturing plant at Franklin, Ohio. Facilities investments include pulp and paper mill expansions at Plattsburgh, New York; Crossett, Arkansas; and Port Hudson, Louisiana as well as a new corrugated container facility at Plano, Texas. Robert Pamplin retires as chairman and is succeeded by Robert Flowerree; Marshall Hahn is named president. Sales top $4 billion, and net income for the year is $215 million.

1978

Georgia-Pacific builds and expands 15 operations this year, including two new Southern pine plywood plants, and completed the Franklin, Ohio, roofing plant. The company announces it will relocate its headquarters to Atlanta, Georgia.

1979

Georgia-Pacific acquires Hudson Pulp and Paper Corporation of Palatka, Florida, which includes pulp and paper production, tissue converting, 550,000 acres of timberlands, two multiwall bag plants and a polyethylene film chemical plant. The company issues floating-rate notes to fund continued expansion and offers transferring employees an 8.5 percent mortgage rate. Sales exceed $5 billion for the first time.

1980

The company begins producing oriented strand board (OSB) at Woodland, Maine and Dudley, North Carolina, and it expands resin manufacturing capacity at Conway, North Carolina. Soaring interest rates begin to cause trouble for G-P, which is heavily in debt.

1981

Georgia-Pacific continues to acquire new facilities, including eight container plants, six resin facilities and the Holly Hill Lumber Company of Holly Hill, South Carolina. The company completes construction of a computerized pine sawmill at Ellabell, Georgia, and a major expansion of the tissue converting facility at Palatka, Florida. The Crossett, Arkansas, chemical plant opens and becomes the first Georgia-Pacific facility to produce fractionated tall oil products and other specialty chemicals. The company's debt now totals $1.66 billion.

1982

Georgia-Pacific moves into its new headquarters building in Atlanta, Georgia. The company acquires a thermosetting resin plant in Elk Grove, California, and expands its Crossett, Arkansas, chemical operations.

1983

Marshall Hahn succeeds Robert Floweree as chairman and CEO. Hahn begins to sell G-P's less profitable businesses to help generate needed cash for the company.

1984

Georgia-Pacific announces a program to focus on expanding pulp and paper operations, moving into higher margin paper products and acquiring the best run mills not already owned by G-P. First steps include conversion and upgrade at Crossett, Arkansas, and Palatka, Florida; installation of a large white paper machine at Port Hudson, Louisiana; and the acquisition of the first of the "Top 10" mills on G-P's wish list: a major containerboard mill at Monticello, Mississippi. The Monticello deal includes 275,000 acres of timberlands and 15 container plants. The company sells its commodity chemicals business to a group of executives, creating Georgia Gulf Corporation.

1985

Georgia-Pacific acquires two sawmills in Virginia and begins production at new oriented strand board plants at Grenada, Mississippi, and Skippers, Virginia. The company sells Exchange Oil & Gas Corporation for $180 million. The United Paperworkers' International Union initiates a major strike at G-P's Crossett, Arkansas, facility, and G-P hires replacement workers until the strike is resolved.

1986

The company purchases five hardboard plants, three molding plants and a kiln-dried hardwood lumber facility. It enters the premium bath tissue market with the introduction of Angel Soft. It also opens a new thermosetting resin facility in Michigan. Sales reach $7 billion, signaling the company's complete recovery from its recent money troubles.

1987

Georgia-Pacific purchases U.S. Plywood for $208 million, including distribution and shipping facilities, five sawmills, a plywood plant and 200,000 acres of timberlands. The company also acquires converting and distribution assets of Erving Distributor Products Company, including two tissue plants. G-P also purchases two hardwood sawmills and two pine sawmills and announces major capacity increases in paper and paperboard product lines. The distribution division begins operating 12 millwork and specialty distribution centers.

1988

Georgia-Pacific acquires Brunswick Pulp & Paper Company for $667 million. Along with three sawmills and more than 500,000 acres of timberlands, the deal gives G-P another mill on its wish list: a pulp and paperboard mill at Brunswick, Georgia. The company also purchases assets of American Forest Products Company at Martell, California, with two sawmills, a particleboard plant and 125,000 acres of timberlands. A second large white paper machine at Port Hudson, Louisiana is completed. Pete Correll leaves Mead to join G-P. The company reforests 100,000 acres of harvested land, planting 34.7 million seedlings. Sales reach $9.5 billion.

1989

Georgia-Pacific announces a cash tender offer for Great Northern Nekoosa Corporation, but current leadership initially fights the proposed merger. Pete Correll, named Executive Vice President of Pulp and Paper, delivers a speech to G-P's pulp and paper leaders that gives the first glimpse of the transformational effect he will have on the company.

1990

The merger of Great Northern Nekoosa Corporation, completed this year, costs G-P $5.4 billion and adds 55 paper mills and paperboard converting plants, 83 paper distribution centers, one plywood plant and two sawmills to G-P's assets. Three of the 55 mills are on G-P's Top 10 wish list: Ashdown, Arkansas; Leaf River, Mississippi; and Cedar Springs, Georgia. Sales reach $12.7 billion.

1991

The company begins to sell nonstrategic assets, starting with two containerboard mills, 19 corrugated packaging plants and related timberlands, and two groundwood paper mills and related timberlands in Maine. Pete Correll is named president.

1992

Georgia-Pacific's continued leadership role in worker safety programs leads to the company becoming the first forest products company to reach Star Level from the Occupational Safety and Health Administration for exemplary safety program at the Crossett, Arkansas, pulp and paper facility.

1993

Georgia-Pacific's renewed focus on environmental responsibility results in a first-of-its-kind agreement with the Department of the Interior to protect the endangered red-cockaded woodpecker on company lands. The company also purchases an engineered lumber mill at Roxboro, North Carolina, and majority ownership of an industrial particleboard facility in Ontario, Canada. G-P sells Butler Paper distribution operations. Marshall Hahn retires, and Pete Correll succeeds him as chairman.

1994

The company begins a multiyear capital investment program focused on growing engineered wood products. It also initiates the Mill Improvement Program to increase efficiency at all G-P mills. The company sells the envelope manufacturing and roofing businesses and begins a major restructuring of the building products distribution business. After years of litigation and scientific research surrounding the Leaf River mill (acquired as part of Great Northern Nekoosa), G-P proves that the mill is not the source of dioxins in the river. The company also enters into a unique land agreement with The Nature Conservancy to protect one of the "Last Great Places" in America, 21,000 acres along the Lower Roanoke River in North Carolina.

1995

Georgia-Pacific begins production of oriented strand board at its Mt. Hope, West Virginia, plant. It purchases two U.S. resin facilities from Dyno Industrier, A.S. G-P's sales reach $14.3 billion. The recovery of the pulp and paper market helps G-P's net income triple this year, from $310 million to $1.018 billion.

1996

The company acquires the gypsum wallboard business of Domtar Inc. for $350 million. Another oriented strand board plant is completed, at Brookneal, Virginia. G-P opens a new recycling facility and recycled linerboard machine at Big Island, Virginia. The company completes a modernization project at the Toledo, Oregon, facility.

1997

Georgia-Pacific completes the sale of its Martell, California, timberlands, sawmill and particleboard plant. In a bold move, G-P begins the spin-off of its timberlands by creating The Timber Company, a separate operating group with its own common stock that tracks the performance and value of the company's timber business; the stock begins trading December 17.

1998

Georgia-Pacific acquires CeCorr, the leading independent producer of corrugated sheets in the U.S. G-P also forms a relationship with Southeast Wood Treating, making Georgia-Pacific a leader in pressure-treated Southern pine. The Timber Company and the U.S. Fish and Wildlife Service renew the landmark agreement to protect endangered red-cockaded woodpecker habitat.

1999

Georgia-Pacific acquires Unisource Worldwide, Inc., the leading independent marketer and distributor of printing and imaging paper, packaging and supply systems in North America, for $1.5 billion. It also forms a joint venture, combining G-P's away-from-home tissue business with Wisconsin Tissue's. The Timber Company completes strategic sale of timberlands in California, Maine and New Brunswick, Canada. G-P's building products sector posts a record operating profit of $1.2 billion. Over the past five years, G-P's Mill Improvement Program has reduced pulp and paper mill costs by $320 million while adding 1,000 tons per day to the company's mill capacity.

2000

On November 27, G-P completes the acquisition of Fort James Corporation and its consumer brands Brawny, Quilted Northern and Dixie for approximately $11 billion, becoming the world's leading manufacturer of tissue products. Company sales reach $22 billion.

2001

Georgia-Pacific begins a major marketing effort to present its consumer-oriented image to the public. The company sells 368,000 tons of commercial tissue capacity to Svenska Cellulosa Aktiebolaget and a portion of its pulp and paper assets to Domtar Inc. G-P completes the sale of The Timber Company to Plum Creek Timber Company, Inc. in a $4 billion transaction.

2002

Georgia-Pacific celebrates its 75th year in business.

Index

Page numbers appear in boldface for illustrations